Moroseta Kitchen Recipes and Stories
from a Modern Puglian Farmhouse

Giorgia Eugenia Goggi

Hardie Grant

BOOKS

CONTENTS

SPRING 26

SUMMER 76

BASICS 230

INTRODUCTION 07
A DAY OF EATING 21
CARLO ON
  MOROSETA KITCHEN 25

AUTUMN 130

WINTER 182

INDEX 248
ACKNOWLEDGEMENTS 254
ABOUT THE AUTHOR 255

INTRODUCTION

I grew up in a family that always considered food to be the
founding element of our togetherness and an expression of
love. Our everyday meals were carefully prepared using seasonal
ingredients, cooked the right way, with an essential, ethical and
elegant approach that I still envy: pasta with butter, Parmesan,
a little black pepper and a few basil leaves torn by hand – shiny,
perfectly emulsified, delicate, but with well-defined aromas, and
passatelli in chicken broth, served on foggy winter evenings, with
a lemon and nutmeg aroma that I could recognise among a thousand.
But holidays or important events, however, were commemorated
with my mother's meticulous preparation of more elaborate dishes;
my memory is dotted with beautiful lunches, picnics in nature and
wonderful Christmas dinners. As a result, I was fascinated by the
wizardy of it, and spent hours reading my mother's great cookery
books like *Pellegrino Artusi* or Ada Boni's *Talisman of Happiness*, losing
myself in descriptions of incredible tortellini, timbales, soufflés,
stuffed duck and orange and raspberry aspic. As an extension
of this sense of occasion, we frequently visited restaurants,
and I remember observing the beautifully laid tables with their
freshly ironed white tablecloths, gazing spellbound at the dessert
trolley, noting what I had eaten the previous time, to make sure I
prioritized the experience of something new rather than indulging
myself with the familiar.

Alongside an education in good food, I also received an education for creativity, and my parents were particularly concerned in raising us broad-mindedly. As children we had the opportunity to express ourselves, to invent games, to turn the house into our stage; we drew on the walls, spun stories and created imaginary worlds. But it was only when I became a teenager that food and creativity merged; I was the sibling who knew how to cook, who was always in charge of grocery shopping and preparing food on weekends with friends. I used to buy lots of cookbooks and magazines, avidly read the history of great chefs and study new culinary techniques. Pastry became my first culinary passion; I started making patisserie at home, buying lots of specialist equipment and trying my hand at more and more complex preparations. But this initial foray didn't lead straight into a career in the kitchen — I was particularly good at school, a model student I dare say, so my parents encouraged me to continue my academic studies. After high school I went to university to study architecture and engineering, hoping that it would combine my academic discipline with my creative spirit. After the first year exams I realised that this was not the case, though, so I pivoted to a design degree, specialising in fashion — another long-standing love.

I started working as an assistant for various fashion magazines while still studying — I wanted to test myself and learn on the job. I spent four years utterly devoting myself to that world, working every hour, including weekends, to find that elusive combination of hard work and creative process, but it wasn't to be. I found myself in an environment that majored on following orders, always being available no matter what, with little respect for those who were learning the ropes. But, despite exhausting days of work with little between flashes and fancy dresses, I would always come home and immediately start cooking to regain my sense of well being. I began to realise that this was the space where I could really express myself, and so my journey into the kitchen began.

Without any previous experience and having never been on a cooking course, I pitched up at some restaurants. A sushi restaurant eventually took me on (perhaps a less obvious entry point, but knowing the chef meant my chances were slightly

better), and so I began my first stage in a kitchen. I did very simple, basic things like cleaning mountains of shrimp for tempura, folding seaweed for rolls or mixing wasabi powder and water; I was happy, I liked the atmosphere of the restaurant, and I got up in the morning ecstatic to go to work — it was a world away from my job in fashion in every way. What followed was two years of bouncing from kitchen to kitchen, gathering knowledge, contacts and shaping my own personal style. I see this period as embued with random twists of fate, where I just let things happen naturally, without forcing anything.

It was the winter of 2016. I was travelling in India and one morning — I still remember everything about that morning — I received an email that I wasn't expecting. Two friends from Milan were writing to me say that a friend of theirs, Carlo, who had recently opened a masseria in Puglia, was looking for a chef, mainly to do breakfasts and take care of the vegetable garden. When I read the name of the masseria, my heart skipped a beat: I knew the place very well. I had been eyeing it for a few months, drooling over the beautiful photos, and had secretly thinking to myself how amazing it would be to hold a residency there. The fact that it was such a high level of design, innovative but also classic, and the small scale of the property — there were only six rooms — made it feel like the perfect next step at the stage I was at in my career. I took it as yet another twist of fate, and accepted the job without hesitation, winding down the collaborations I was doing in Milan.

Six months later, in June 2017, I arrived at Masseria Moroseta after driving through the length of Italy for the first time in my life. After no more than two weeks of working together, I realised that Carlo and I had a special connection. We liked the same things, we worked in a complementary way — I had found the balance of hard work and creativity I was looking for. There was no professional kitchen, just a beautiful home kitchen with a comfortable sofa, a television (!!) and simple, homely equipment. After the first season, we decided to make some modifications to make the set up more suitable for all the experimenting I wanted to do. We also expanded the kitchen garden, taking the whole field in front of the kitchen terrace, so that I could easily go back and forth if they needed fresh herbs or vegetables.

From that first day, Carlo gave me great freedom; I chose the suppliers, ingredients and menus by myself. Having that enormous trust from him was exactly what I needed to focus on the project and exploring the potential of my creativity, giving everything I had to give at that moment. I think we both felt after a few weeks that there was something magical, something hard to explain but which became evident in our day-to-day life. So, we decided to go on for the winter season, then the spring season, and so on. Now, almost eight years later, I still believe that it was always meant to be. Before I moved to Puglia and started my adventure at Masseria Moroseta, I had a hard time defining myself as a chef, and I still see myself as more of a person that's passionate about food who moves freely between research, self-expression, communication, contamination with other fields, merging all this with the sustainable dimension of restaurant and farm. My focus is a personal quest; it is not dictated by fashions or market dynamics, just by the possibility of being able to reinvent and amaze, and building a relationship of trust with customers, colleagues, and suppliers.

Living in Puglia all came about by chance, but in a short time I realised that it was the only place I could realise the project that I was struggling to focus on until then. Puglia is rich in traditions, rooted and radical in its attachment to its ways. All this rustic simplicity and authenticity of meaning was enlightening for me. In Puglia, all families have their habits: fresh pasta made by grandmothers, the olive harvest all together, the ritual of tomato sauce at the end of August. There is a strong sense of community, and the villages are still full of life. Everyone helps each other, everyone knows each other, in the morning they meet at the bar for coffee and the day's chatter.

The beauty, too, is extreme: the blue sea, the red earth, the centuries-old olive trees, the quality of the ingredients, the cultural and historical depth. It is hard to bring everything into focus, there is too much to see and discover. You have to get to know it slowly, you have to learn its language and customs in order to get to the real Puglia – that of small villages, peasant traditions, patron saints and endless family lunches; this strong foundation gave me confidence, I felt rooted and safe in that place, protected and at the same time free to create. I have this vivid memory of when, in my first summer in Puglia, I ate an apricot.

It was an almost Proustian moment. It was the taste of the apricots from my childhood, the ones that came from the farmer in the village where I spent my holidays; small, firm, and perfect.

Many guests have told me that my way of cooking very much reflects the aesthetics of Moroseta; simple, clean, but at the same time refined, not obvious, with hints of Puglia, but definitely not local. It's by no means a conscious thing: I simply started doing what I wanted. It was the first time I was running a kitchen on my own and not following someone's orders, so I began with everything I had not been able to do in previous kitchens, cooking exactly what I had in my head, what I really loved, and what I would have liked if I had been one of my own guests. Next, I researched producers in the area, getting to know them personally, listening to their stories and having them explain the seasonality of the ingredients to me. One of the elements that made me fall in love, that made me think that Puglia could really be the right place to develop that personal project I had been waiting to do all my life, was this early engagement with the local ingredients – to be able to cook with them was the ultimate privilege. And being in the the countryside was enlightening; I gained the space to detangle all my thoughts.

Usually, it is me who arrives in the morning with some new idea, which I have dreamt up or read in a book, but then everything comes to life by talking to the team – tests are made, samples are tasted, discussions take place, ideas are exchanged and something good comes out, often diametrically opposed to the initial concept. I am so appreciative of this process, having been alone in the kitchen until 2020, at which point we realised we needed to expand. Our menu starts with the ingredients of this place, selecting them with care and love, but then what happens is a mosaic of suggestions that unfold differently each time.

As much as I am the author of this book and chef in the kitchen, I firmly believe that this is one hundred per cent a collective project. It is made up of all the people who have passed through our kitchen, our suppliers, the guests we are lucky enough to have and who renew their trust in us every time they sit down at our table. Without the fundamental contribution they have made, none of this would have happened; it's like an extraordinary orchestra.

A DAY OF EATING

BREAKFAST

Breakfast is our business card, the way we welcome guests and introduce ourselves – it is as much of an important meal as any other. We begin with small dishes with fruit and vegetables, seasoned simply with fresh herbs, honey and lemon, a little bit suspended between sweet and savoury. A baked treat always follows, be it cake, croissants or fresh-from-the-oven biscotti. And then there's cheese: just-made ricotta, still warm, mozzarella or small burratas that we simply serve with olive oil and fresh herbs.

For months I concentrated on refining our egg cooking techniques; as we have our own hens, I wanted them to be simple but perfect. The omelette in particular I obsessed over for months. In addition to eggs, we also make à la minute desserts, such as pancakes with fruit preserves, warm and super creamy risolatte, spicy porridge in the winter months, toast with whipped ricotta and honey, now a bestseller. I like the idea that our guests are served something different every day, the common thread being that each element represents something perfectly in season and of the moment.

LUNCH

Lunch is by far the most freestyle service we do – in eight years of Moroseta Kitchen, we have never had a previously agreed lunch menu. We usually improvise according to what we have available and also, above all, according to how much time we have that day because lunch arrives just when we have just finished sorting out the whole breakfast line and start organising all the work to be done during the day for dinner. The preparation of lunch has to be quick – no more than half an hour – and have fresh and light dishes, considering it swiftly follows a fairly indulgent breakfast. It centres on sauces and dressings that allow us to quickly season and transform fresh garden vegetables into perfect small plates to share with good bread. After the vegetable dishes usually comes a pasta or soup, as simple and basic as a classic spaghetti al pomodoro or a lentil soup with croutons and crème fraîche. Lunch always ends with gelato, served straight up.

In the afternoon there is always fresh fruit from the garden: large bowls of grapes, tangerines, juicy peaches, cherries and crisp apples, depending on the season. The true country merenda. I'm usually the one who makes the afternoon cakes. It's an activity that relaxes and reconnects, and I love placing them on the bar and seeing guests help themselves to the offerings.

APERITIVO

At 6.30 p.m. the aperitif hour strikes and our bar fills with the golden light of sunset. We serve simple drinks with little twists made in Moroseta Kitchen, such as gin and tonic with herb and lemon syrup or a variation of spritz with garden fruit shrub. To accompany the drinks, we always offer our own taralli and olives. Sometimes the kitchen brings out freshly made focaccia, semolina crackers or small bbq skewers. We love the moment of the aperitivo, so quintessentially Italian and so symbolic of the feeling of being on holiday. We like it so much that twice a month, in the summer season, we invite wine producers or mixologists to talk to our guests and create an event around aperitivo, accompanied by informal, unusual small plates from the kitchen.

DINNER

Dinner is the real core around which everything revolves. We only have dinner four times a week, as we also like the masseria to have quiet evenings where everything is peaceful and guests are free to sit by the pool until sunset, drink a bottle of wine undisturbed or play cards under the pergola. Dinner is about seven courses, and I say 'about' because the structure also changes often.

Over the years, we have given more and more space to vegetable ingredients, especially from our own garden or from trusted small producers in the area. We like to start with a course simply called 'bread service' – a thick slice of our sourdough bread accompanied by our own extra-virgin olive oil, small marinated vegetables, pickles, hummus or fresh cheese – it is a convivial, simple, honest start and very representative of our approach of always putting the ingredient at the heart of everything.

I like to bring the first course out myself and say a few words; I think it's a nice way to welcome guests, creating an easy, family atmosphere right away. We continue with a couple of starters, which can be a small crudo of fish or a fresh, acidic vegetable course. Then comes a primo – what Italian menu would be without a primo? I tried to take it off a few times, but I felt I was betraying our roots and at the same time the customers also really appreciated our expressions of risotto, pasta or ravioli.

The main course is served in several small shared plates: a small portion of meat or fish, accompanied by seasonal side dishes and sauces, to be combined and eaten freely, experimenting and sharing, just like at home. Dessert always has some gelato in it that's for sure. I like to use mainly seasonal fruit and sharp acidity, after a good number of courses the palate needs freshness and verve to continue the journey.

TO FINISH

We finish with an herbal tea, hot or cold depending on the season, accompanied by a small treat, such as a small tartlet, pate de fruit or choux. At the end of the dinner if guests are still hungry or want to indulge a little more, there is a chance to try some local cheese with fruit bread; we work with some really talented cheesemakers who make blue and mature cheeses that are perfect to end the dinner.

Dinners take place four nights a week and have always been held with blind menus, which means the guest only finds out what they are going to eat when they sit down at the table, we never communicate the menu in advance. First of all because we don't want expectations to be created about it – it's certainly better to be surprised and guided than to arrive already with precise ideas in your head. And secondly, because we often make last-minute variations, so often there is a big difference from the morning briefing to the final result.

Dinner often closes with the guests – who initially did not know each other – chatting, sharing wine andcontinuing the conversation, even if the service is over. I am always enchanted by the ability of food to unite, to create bonds, tell stories and transform into something else.

CARLO ON MOROSETA KITCHEN

Masseria Moroseta is aytypical. I didn't grow up in Puglia, and it was designed by British architect Andrew Trotter, and so I knew the food had to reflect how this place is so different from the hundreds of masserias in Puglia. When Moroseta first opened, the food offering I had felt like a mismatch; it was relatively traditional, but all that changed when Giorgia arrived.

A friend put me in touch with her initially. In the early days, Moroseta was a bed and breakfast, and Giorgia had agreed to come for two months to cook for the guests – it was just myself at that point, so she also ended up helping me with check in and check out, too. We spent all of our time together, and almost instantly, I realised that I wanted her to stay. Her approach was so fresh – her gentle creativity, respect for ingredients and lightness of touch worked in such perfect harmony with the surroundings. It's now been eight years, and Giorgia is my right arm – she is of course the heart of the kitchen, but a part of everything that Moroseta does.

I remember the dish she cooked that made me not only realise that she had to stay at Moroseta, but also cemented the idea that we expand our offering to dinners. It was a pasta mista, which essentially is the scraps of leftover pasta dough once pasta shapes have been made. She cooked it in a fish broth with coconut milk and spices. It was truly special; Giorgia can be very minimal in her approach, but her food is also comforting and full of flavour.

I like to think that her journey as a chef, growing in confidence, is in part due to the freedom she's had here to experiment and explore. She cooks with the best

produce of the region, but gives it a completely new spin. We needed a different point of view, and that's what the food brings. But we also share a love of traditional cooking; we both grew up in the north, and have fond memories of the ingredients that our grandmothers used. Vinegar, for example, is always present in Giorgia's food, and it's a reflection of the food we ate in our childhoods.

It's pure freedom to be here with no rules, and we know that our guests stay time and time again because they are looking for something different. Each year, we try to build on what we have created; an extended vegetable garden and a larger area for barbecuing, for example. We started out with breakfast (I believe it to be the best in Italy) and then had small dinners for guests here and there, before opening it up to external diners, and finally workshops and events. At the moment, we can seat up to 45 people in summer, but at the height of the season, we have a waiting list of three hundred.

The most important thing about our friendship is trust and intuition – I've never asked her what she's cooking or looked at a menu in advance, because I've always trusted her. She's spontaneous, and it inspires me to be the same. I sometimes spend the evenings with her in the kitchen during service, because I know it makes her happy when i'm there too, tasting things, changing dishes as the service progresses. We are both truly involved in everything. I am always amazed at how in the morning, when we go for a walk in the fields, she will forage ingredients that then will become something extraordinarily special on the dinner menu that evening.

01 SPRING

I vividly remember my first spring here in Puglia, in 2018. For a city girl who grew up amidst concrete and traffic, spring was simply about the temperatures getting warmer and little else; it was incredible to experience the radically changing landscape, endless expanses of flowers, almond trees as bright white clouds.

At the beginning of March, while we are waiting for the kitchen garden to spring to life, we set to foraging for our ingredients: rocket as spicy as wasabi; sorrel; borage plants with beautiful blue flowers; wild garlic; bronze fennel and asparagus. As a result, spring cooking is very poetic, delicate and graceful. Techniques are simpler. There is more time spent finely slicing strawberries and shelling peas than over a stove. The menu is a hymn to rebirth and the awakening of nature.

GRILLED ASPARAGUS,
GREMOLATA, TAHINI SAUCE

Serves 6

As soon as it becomes available, asparagus is a constant presence in our kitchen. It is simply too good not to use, and we prepare it in many ways, featuring it on breakfast, lunch and dinner tasting menus.

Grilling asparagus is one of the first things I learned to do in a professional kitchen. Despite its simplicity, it can give a sublime depth of flavour; the key is to get the right consistency between cooked and crunchy, and ensure a nice even caramelisation for a smoky aroma and sweet, mineral taste. If you have the option, grilling asparagus on a barbecue is ideal, but a cast-iron griddle or a blow torch will also do the trick.

The most important thing is to select good-quality asparagus that is fresh, local and organically grown. The spears should be bright green, unmarked and firm, with crispy tips.

Ingredients

1 kg (2 lb 4 oz) asparagus spears
40 g (2 oz) olive oil
sea salt flakes

For the gremolata
1 mint spring
1 parsley sprig
4 anchovies
zest of 1 lemon and juice of ½
drizzle of Garlic Oil (page 244)

To finish
100 g (3½ oz) Tahini Sauce (page 238)
70 g (2¼ oz) Savoury Crumble (page 238)
mixed herbs and flowers
extra virgin olive oil, for drizzling

Method

1. Prepare the asparagus: Wash the asparagus well and pat dry with kitchen paper. Taking one spear at a time, gently pull it until it breaks. It will naturally break at the point where the tender part meets the hard part. If the spears are large, you may need to peel them slightly at the base. You will need 6 medium-sized asparagus spears per serving, plus 12 thinner ones for the gremolata.

2. Make the gremolata: Finely slice the 12 thinner spears, including the tips, and place in a small bowl. Finely chop the mint, parsley and anchovies. Scatter the lemon zest over the chopped asparagus, then add the freshly chopped herbs and anchovies to the bowl. Squeeze over the lemon juice and top with a good drizzle of Garlic Oil. Mix well and leave to rest for a few minutes. It is best not to add salt to this, as the anchovies will release a salty flavour.

3. Grill the asparagus: Preheat the barbecue to medium heat. Drizzle the remaining asparagus spears with oil and season with salt. Cook them on the barbecue for about 5–7 minutes, turning often until they are evenly cooked and browned, keeping them at least 10 cm (4 in) above the hot coals.

4. Assemble: Divide the Tahini Sauce between 6 flat plates, spreading a good dollop on each dish. Arrange a portion of grilled asparagus on top of the sauce, slightly overlapping the spears.

5. Taste the gremolata for seasoning; it should be tangy and flavourful. Adjust as needed, and pour a generous spoonful on to each plate. Add a little savoury crumble to the side of each plate, and garnish with the herbs. Finish with a few drops of extra virgin olive oil and a pinch of flaky salt.

SMOKED SPRING ONIONS,
CHESTNUT HONEY, HAZELNUTS

Serves 6

I have to be honest, when I make this, I don't use ordinary spring onions (scallons); I use *sponsali*, an indigenous wonder I discovered on a trip to the market a few years ago. Also known as '*porraie* onions', they are like partly grown onion bulbs, and are a rather common (if niche!) crop in Puglia. Unlike the spring onion, the *sponsale* is characterised by a sweetness that makes it particularly suitable for braising; it is used to stuff a typical focaccia called calzone. To counteract its natural sweetness, we cook it in over the barbecue to give it a smoky note and concentrate its flavours. Once the burned outer peels have been removed the *sponsale* reveals itself in all its glory, with a silky, irresistible texture.

Ingredients

18 small spring onions (scallions) or
    sponsali (around 2 kg)
100 g (33/4 oz) hazelnuts
120 g (4¼ oz) Brown Butter (page 233)
25 g (1 oz/scant 2 tablespoons) Carpione
    Vinegar (page 244)
60 g (2 oz/3 tablespoons) chestnut honey
salt and freshly ground black pepper

To serve
chive flowers
sprig of thyme, leaves picked

Method

1. Prepare the spring onions: Preheat the barbecue to high. In the meantime, remove any soil from the spring onions, removing the roots if they are particularly dirty, but leaving the outer layers intact.

2. Cook them over a high flame for 20–25 minutes, until they are well browned and you can feel that the inside has softened by poking them with a skewer. If they are still firm inside, you can finish cooking them in the oven for up to 20 minutes at 170°C fan (340°F/gas 5) wrapping them in foil to avoid darkening them further.

3. Take one spring onion at a time and place it on a cutting board. Carefully run a sharp knife down its length, piercing the first two layers but trying not to go too deep. Open the first two layers like a book, leaving the inside part whole. Touch the spring onion to determine its consistency; you will find that part is tender, and part is more fibrous. Remove the tender part and trim into a portion about 15 cm (6 in) long. Keep all the trimmings aside, including the two blackened outer layers.

4. Repeat with the remaining spring onions. Neatly arrange all the tender pieces on a tray lined with baking parchment, and set aside until later.

5. Make the spring onion powder: Place all the spring onion scraps back on the barbecue and close the lid, allowing them to smoke in the residual heat for 20 minutes. Once smoked, dehydrate them in a dehydrator at 70°C (158°F) or in a low oven for 3–6 hours until dry and crispy.

6. Transfer to a blender and pulverise until you have fragrant smoked spring onion powder. Keep in an airtight container.

7. Toast the hazelnuts: Preheat the oven to 160°C fan (320°F/gas 4). Scatter the nuts on to a baking tray and toast for 8 minutes until golden and fragrant. Remove from the oven, chop and set aside.

8. Warm the spring onions: Pour half the Brown Butter over the spring onion portions and season with salt. Place in the oven for 8 minutes to warm through; they should not brown.

9. Remove from the oven and spray with the Carpione Vinegar, then drizzle over the chestnut honey, brushing it to ensure it is distributed evenly. Taste and adjust seasoning if necessary; the spring onions should taste really well dressed and irresistible.

10. Assemble: Divide the spring onions between six warm plates, using an offset spatula to keep them nicely lined up. Drizzle with more Brown Butter, then scatter over the toasted hazelnuts and herbs. Finish with a good pinch of burned spring onion powder.

11. Serve immediately with warm bread.

ON ASPARAGUS

In Puglia, the first asparagus usually arrives in mid-March, exactly when our kitchen reopens after the holidays and we all start to wake up from the winter slumber, enchanted by the idea that spring and sunshine are finally on the way.

The flavour of asparagus is herbaceous, rich and slightly sulphurous, reminiscent of the taste of green walnuts. Although asparagus is usually boiled, I believe it reaches its full potential when subjected to bolder cooking methods, such as grilling, cooking over coals, or sautéing in a really hot pan. It is also excellent raw, when the spears are super fresh and crunchy. Sliced thinly and seasoned simply, they are able to show off their herbaceous flavour and super-crisp texture – a true ode to spring.

In our area, it is common to find thin and absolutely delicious wild asparagus; it grows abundantly close to dry stone walls in the countryside after the spring rains. Local ladies prepare it in frittatas enriched with Pecorino cheese, stale bread and mint. To clean asparagus effectively, simply take a spear, look to see where the tender part meets the fibrous base, and snap it in just the right place. This can only be done when they are really fresh; if they are quite large and therefore more fibrous, you may need to lightly peel the base with a vegetable peeler. Any peelings and scraps can be used to flavour a vegetable broth, which can then form the base of a risotto or spring minestrone, for example.

ASPARAGUS AND EGGS

I know, pure avant-garde, but how could we not mention this classic and incredibly good combination? When asparagus is in season, it becomes the inseparable companion to our hens' eggs, proudly served at breakfast every day. I prefer my eggs soft-boiled with some asparagus sautéed in brown butter and topped with a cloud of freshly grated Parmesan cheese: the best breakfast of the year.

ASPARAGUS AND SEAWEED

The rich, sweet and enveloping flavour of asparagus loves the oceanic and mineral notes of seaweed. Try serving your asparagus in a dashi broth made with kombu seaweed, or drizzle it with a hollandaise sauce and garnish with crispy dulse flakes.

ASPARAGUS AND SEAFOOD

For the same reason, combining asparagus with seafood is also very successful, with the additional benefit that the sweet, melt-in-the-mouth component of fish exquisitely contrasts with the earthy notes of asparagus. We especially recommend pairing it with oysters, langoustines and prawns.

ASPARAGUS AND NUTS

Having a natural hint of walnut to its flavour profile, asparagus pairs well with this and other types of nuts for a delicious fat-on-fat overlay. Try serving yours with our Almond Mayo (page 232) or Almond Emulsion (page 232).

SPRING GARDEN SALAD

Serves 6

After the winter, during which our garden is quieter and not very productive, spring heralds the moment we can finally have fun and enjoy all the little tender leaves that begin to grow in abundance. This salad does not hide any genius ideas, but it is a simple and sincere tribute to the beauty of our garden. We compose it daily, picking what is available, mixing sweet, delicate and bitter leaves with herbs, so that each bite has its own distinct and pronounced taste. Laura, with her poetic forager spirit, is undoubtedly the best person for the job. Every day, she visits the vegetable garden in front of the kitchen, and returns with well-organised trays of herbs, flowers and small fruits, which are then lightly dressed with an ethereal vinaigrette that binds it all together.

Ingredients

300 g (10½ oz) mixed salad leaves, as many
    varieties as possible, preferably small-leaved
    (ideally butter lettuce, sorrel, rocket, mizuna,
    watercress and dandelion)
60 g (2 oz) mixed herbs and edible flowers
    (ideally mint, onion flowers, rosemary flowers,
    fennel, Greek basil, verbena, oxalis, nasturtium)
100 g (3½ oz) small strawberries, halved (a mix of
    ripe and unripe)

For the vinaigrette
35 g (1¼ oz) Elderflower Vinegar (page 74)
10 g (½ oz/½ tablespoon) honey
5 g (¼ oz/1 teaspoon) salt
10 g (½ oz/2 teaspoons) lemon juice
60 g (2 oz/4 tablespoons) extra virgin olive oil
40 g (1½ oz/ 2½ tablespoons) grapeseed oil

Method

1. Prepare the salad leaves: Carefully rinse the salad leaves under cold running water, then spin with a salad spinner, a handful at a time (don't overcrowd the spinner, or it will take much longer). Arrange the leaves in layers in a container, separating the layers with kitchen paper to absorb any residual moisture.

2. If the herbs are clean and do not have any traces of soil, I usually prefer not to wash them, so as not to spoil them or compromise the aromatic component. If they are dirty, you can proceed as follows: fill a bowl with cold water, immerse the herbs, moving them a little with your hands so that the residual soil comes off. Drain using a perforated ladle and place on a tray lined with kitchen paper. Leave to dry for a few minutes, without pressing.

3. Make the vinaigrette: In a small bowl, combine the vinegar with the honey, salt and lemon, and stir well. Slowly add the oils, emulsifying with a whisk. Transfer to a bottle and keep in the refrigerator until needed.

4. Assemble and dress: In a large bowl, combine the salad leaves, herbs and strawberries (see Chef's Notes). Pour over some dressing and, with gentle movements from the bottom up, distribute it evenly throughout the salad. Taste and add more dressing if necessary. Divide the salad between six shallow bowls and serve immediately.

Chef's Notes:

Be gentle: Dressing the salad is the most delicate part. Choose a wide bowl, much wider than necessary, so that you don't crowd the leaves. This will keep them airy, crisp and light. Pour in the dressing a little at a time; salt and acidity tend to 'cook' the leaves, so it's better not to overdo it; let the different leaves express their characters. It is important to be able distinguish the different flavours; the dressing should simply bind them together, not cover them.

MONKS BEARD, PICKLED GARLIC, CANDIED CITRUS

Serves 6

The name alone should be enough to win you over; how can you fail to love a vegetable with a name as poetic as monk's beard? Also known as *agretti*, it belongs to the chard and spinach family, and is characterised by thread-like leaves that are reminiscent of chives, but thinner and not hollow. It has a pleasantly sour, slightly bitter and very mineral taste, and may remind you a little of seaweed or samphire. In this simple side dish, we have tried to give it its own importance, taking care to maintain texture and colour, and seasoning it with small touches of candied citrus, pickled garlic and sumac.

Ingredients

600 g (1 lb 5 oz) monk's beard
5 garlic cloves
200 g (7 oz/scant 1 cup) rice vinegar
40 g (1½ oz/3 tablespoons) sugar
60 g (2 oz/generous ⅓ cup) white sesame seeds
70 g (2¼ oz) Candied Citrus Paste (page 234)
25 g (1 oz) sumac

For the toasted sesame vinaigrette
35 g (1¼ oz/generous 2 tablespoons) rice vinegar
5 g (¼ oz/1 teaspoon) shoyu soy sauce
10 g (½ oz/½ tablespoon) honey
10 g (½ oz/2 teaspoons) lemon juice
50 g (2 oz/¼ cup) extra virgin oil
25 g (scant 2 tablespoons) toasted sesame oil
20 g (generous 1 tablespoon) Garlic Oil (page 244)

Method

1. Prepare the monk's beard: Clean the monk's beard by removing the reddish roots and any woody parts. Wash and allow to drain for a few minutes.

2. Bring a pan of salted water to the boil. Add the monk's beard and boil for 3 minutes until firm but tender. Drain and transfer straight into a bowl of iced water to stop further cooking and maintain the bright green colour. Drain in a colander and spread out on a tray lined with kitchen paper to soak up any remaining water.

3. Pickle the garlic: Slice the garlic cloves very thinly using a mandoline (watch your fingers!). In a small saucepan over a medium heat, combine the vinegar and sugar and bring to a gentle boil. Once boiling, take the pan off the heat. Add the garlic slices and leave to stand.

4. Make the vinaigrette: In a small bowl, mix together the vinegar, soy, honey and lemon. Slowly add the oils, using a whisk to emulsify. Transfer to a squeezing bottle.

5. Toast the sesame seeds and assemble: Preheat the oven to 160°C fan (320°F/gas 4). Spread out the sesame seeds on a baking tray and toast for 8 minutes until golden and fragrant. (Watch out for the oven fan; if it is powerful, the sesame is likely to fly off the tray!)

6. With patience, divide the monk's beard into six neat bundles; this will make plating easier. Take the first bundle and starting from the outer edge, shape it into a spiral shape, then place in a shallow bowl. Repeat the with rest.

7. Season generously with the vinaigrette and a pinch of salt. Garnish each bowl with slices of pickled garlic, small dots of citrus paste (using a small piping bag or squeezing bottle), a pinch of sumac and some toasted sesame seeds. Serve immediately.

PEA, WASABI,
MASCARPONE TART

Makes 12

One day, talking to a colleague, I described this dish as a small snack that I could imagine Marie Antoinette enjoying before sitting down to dinner. After pages and pages in which I profess the beauty of nature in its rawest and most authentic state, here, I ask you to place the peas one by one with the use of surgical tweezers; there is little consistency in this, but when one feels free to express oneself, sometimes the results can be discordant, so I hope you can forgive this precise and slightly maddening vein that characterises me.

You will need 12 × 4 cm (1½ in) tartlet moulds.

Ingredients

220 g (7¾ oz) Pasta Frolla (page 239)
plain (all-purpose) flour, for dusting
200 g (7 oz) mascarpone
65 g (2¼ oz) Greek-style yoghurt
7 g (¼ oz) wasabi paste
5 g (¼ oz/1 teaspoon) salt
300 g (10½ oz) freshly shelled peas
12 small chive flowers
sea salt flakes

Method

1. Make the pastry cases: Using a rolling pin, roll out the shortcrust pastry until about 3 mm (⅛ in) thick, trying to use as little flour for dusting as possible. Leave to rest for 15 minutes, then cut out rounds using a 5 cm (2 in) circular cutter. Prick each round with a fork, then use them to line the tartlet moulds, pressing the dough evenly into the moulds and taking care not to deform the pastry. Transfer to the refrigerator for 1 hour to stabilise the dough.

2. Preheat the oven to 160°C fan (320°F/gas 4) and bake the tart cases for 12 minutes until golden and crisp. Cool on a cooling rack, then transfer to an airtight container until needed.

3. Prepare the wasabi mascarpone filling: In a stand mixer fitted with a flat beater attachment, combine the mascarpone, yoghurt, wasabi and salt, and whip for 5 minutes until smooth and a little airy. Transfer into a piping bag and keep in the fridge.

4. Blanch the peas: Bring a saucepan of salted water to the boil. Add the peas and blanch for about 2 minutes, then drain and immediately transfer into a bowl of iced water to stop cooking and retain their bright green colour.

5. Drain in a colander and spread out on a tray lined with paper towels to soak up any remaining water. Transfer to a container and keep cool until needed.

6. Assemble: These tartlets should be assembled just a few minutes before serving. If they are made too far in advance, the crust risks becoming moist and crumbling. Spoon a generous dollop of wasabi mascarpone into each pastry case, trying to achieve a semi-spherical and fairly tall shape; this will be the structure on which the peas will rest.

7. Arm yourself with patience and tweezers and, starting from the bottom, begin to arrange the peas until the entire surface of the wasabi mascarpone is evenly covered. Lightly brush with olive oil and garnish with a pinch of flaky salt and a small chive flower, and serve immediately.

SEMOLINA, FENNEL, OLIVE OIL CRACKERS,
WHIPPED RICOTTA, SPICY HONEY, BEE POLLEN

Serves 6

These crackers are purely addictive; we had to find a secret place to store them because people who kept eating them on the sly (I won't mention names, but you know who you are!). It's inspired by tarallo dough, the quintessential snack in Puglia. Rich in olive oil and white wine, it is crumbly, salty, and perfect at any time. The whipped ricotta cheese makes the perfect partner: soft and airy, it plays really well with the crunchiness of the crackers. We often serve this simple combination to start the meal in spring with garden crudités, pickles or peas and fresh broad beans served in their pods.

Ingredients

For the crackers
7 g (¼ oz) ground wild fennel seeds
250 g (8¾ oz) durum wheat flour, preferably
    Senatore Cappelli
250 g (8¾ oz) whole durum wheat semolina
10 g (½ oz) salt
165 g (5¾ oz/⅔ cup) dry white wine
150 g (5¼ oz/⅗ cup) extra virgin olive oil
35 g (½ oz/2 tablespoons) water

For the whipped ricotta
500 g (1 lb 2oz) fresh sheep's milk ricotta
100 g (3½ oz)r mascarpone
50 g (2 oz/3 tablespoons) cream
50 g (2 oz/scant ¼ cup) yoghurt
5 g (¼ oz/1 teaspoon) salt

To serve
Bay Leaf Oil (page 243)
Spicy Honey (page 237)
nasturtium flowers
fresh pollen
pickles and fresh vegetables

Method

1. Make the crackers: Toast the fennel seeds in a small frying pan over a low heat for 4 minutes until golden and fragrant. Pound with a pestle and mortar, then pass through a sieve to obtain a fine powder.

2. In the bowl of a stand mixer fitted with a dough hook, combine the flours, ground fennel seeds and salt. With the mixer running on a medium speed, slowly pour in the wine, oil and water. Knead for 5–8 minutes until smooth and elastic. Cover the dough with cling film (plastic wrap) and leave to rest for at least 3 hours in the refrigerator.

3. When you are ready to bake, preheat the oven to 210°C fan (410°F/gas 8). Divide the dough into 5 portions and flatten lightly with a rolling pin. Roll out each to a thickness of 2 mm (1⁄16 in), using a pasta machine if you have one. Place each sheet of dough on a separate baking tray.

4. Lightly brush with olive oil and a pinch of salt, then bake for 10–15 minutes until evenly golden. Transfer to cooling racks to cool, then keep in an airtight container.

5. Make the whipped ricotta: Start by draining the ricotta to remove as much whey as possible. To do this, wrap the ricotta in a clean piece of muslin (cheese cloth), then place it in a colander set over a bowl. Place something very heavy on top, and leave to drain for an hour. It should lose about 20 per cent of its weight, depending on how fresh it is.

6. Remove the drained ricotta from the cloth and place in the bowl of a stand mixer. Add the mascarpone, cream, yoghurt and salt. Whisk for a few minutes until the mixture is light and airy. Be careful not to over-whip, as this could make it separate. Transfer to a piping bag and keep chilled.

7. Assemble: This is a sharing dish, so we usually serve it in one bowl per two people. As this serves six, chill three bowls for half an hour before serving. Place a nice generous dollop of whipped ricotta in each dish. Lightly press the centre with the back of a teaspoon, and fill the resulting hollow with bay leaf oil. Drizzle spicy honey over the top and finish with a pinch of salt, a few nasturtium petals and a scatter of fresh pollen.

8. Serve with the crackers, along with some pickles and fresh seasonal vegetables.

BARBECUED OYSTERS,
SPICY STRAWBERRY DRESSING

Serves 6

In the Gargano, north of Puglia, it is possible to find small oysters grown in the Varano Lagoon, which lies within a natural reserve. This rare variety is characterised by a sweet, iodised and mineral flavour. They are excellent simply eaten raw, but we could not resist the temptation to give them a different treatment. Here, they are barbecued for few minutes, unopened, so that they gently steam in their own juices, intensifying their flavour and giving them a pleasantly meaty texture. To contrast with this intense seafood taste, we pair them with a dressing of sweet and spicy strawberries that make each bite complex and succulent. We like to serve these during *aperitivo*, as a small welcome from the kitchen.

Ingredients

12 oysters
rock salt, to serve
60 g (2 oz) Brown Butter (page 233)

For the dressing
180 g (6½ oz) strawberries
30 g (1 oz) Pickled Celery (page 187)
20 g (¾ oz/generous 1 tablespoon) Spicy Vinegar
    (page 245)
8 g (¼ oz/1½ teaspoons) apple cider vinegar
4 g (¼ oz) smoked chilli flakes
20 g (¾ oz/1½ tablespoons) sugar
salt

Method

1. Make the dressing: Wash the strawberries and chop them into 5 mm (¼ in) dice. Very finely dice the Pickled Celery. Combine the strawberries and Pickled Celery in a bowl, then stir in the vinegars, chilli flakes and sugar. Season with a pinch of salt, mix well and leave to macerate for 15 minutes.

2. Cook the oysters: Preheat the barbecue to high heat. Cook the oysters for about 8 minutes; you will notice that the upper shell rises slightly due to the steam that has formed inside. Once cooked, open the oysters and keep the more concave half of the shell.

3. Assemble: Prepare small plates with coarse rock salt; this will make the perfect base on which to place the oysters.

4. Season each oyster with a generous teaspoon of the dressing, taking care to include both the fruit and the juices that will have been released during resting. Finish each one with a drizzle of Brown Butter and serve immediately.

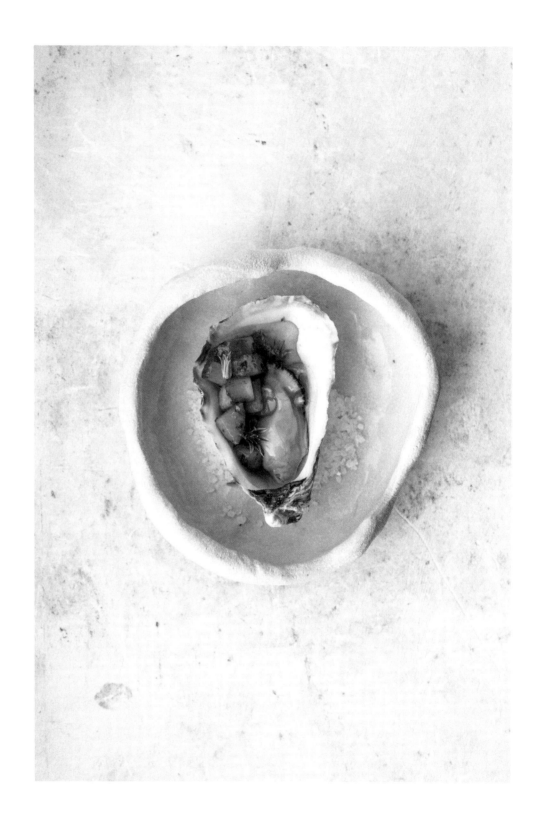

SQUID TARTARE,
WILD SORREL SAUCE

Serves 6

From March onwards, the fields around the farm are
covered with wild sorrel – and I am not talking about
small bushes, but entire wavy expanses where this wild
variety takes up every bit of space possible. It looks like
a clover, consisting of three heart-shaped leaves, which
are very tender and characterised by a strong lemon-like
flavour. Every part of the plant is edible, and it has a long
history of culinary use in ancient cultures. Since we have
a lot of it, we use it as a salad leaf, as an aromatic herb,
to add acidity and to make a delicious green gelato.
In this case, we made a sauce from it to balance a squid
tartare, for a very interesting play of textures and flavours.

Ingredients

6 small squid (120–150 g/4¼–5 oz each)
35 g (2 oz/2 tablespoons) extra virgin olive oil
Garlic Oil (page 244)
salt

For the sauce
250 g (9 oz/1 cup) Greek-style yoghurt
70 g (2¼ oz) concentrated Fish Broth (page 241)
7 g (¼ oz) colatura
70 g (2¼ oz) fresh sorrel, plus extra to serve
4 g (¼ oz/scant 1 teaspoon) salt
7 g (¼ oz/1½ teaspoons) lemon juice

Method

1. Prepare the squid tartare: Clean the squid
    thoroughly. The tentacles can be kept for other
    uses; the clean, skinless tubes are sufficient for
    this recipe. Blot well with paper and remove any
    membranes.

2. Cut one side of the first tube so that it opens
    completely and lies flat. Starting from the larger
    side, slice it into thin strips about 3 mm (⅛ in)
    thick, then slice in the opposite direction to make
    a tartare. Do not just chop several times with the
    knife; it is essential to have a clean, sharp cut to
    obtain a silky, firm texture. Chopping too much
    risks making the squid slimy and sticky.

3. Repeat with the remaining squid. You will need
    about 45 g (1¾ oz) of squid tartare per serving.
    Store in the refrigerator until needed.

4. Make the sauce: Combine all the sauce ingredients
    in a blender and blend for a couple of minutes.
    Pass through a muslin (cheesecloth), then taste
    for seasoning and adjust as needed.

5. Assemble: Dress the squid tartare with the extra
    virgin olive oil, a few drops of garlic oil and a pinch
    of salt. Divide it between six cold bowls, placing the
    tartare on one side of each bowl, trying to give it a
    semi-circular shape using the back of a spoon.

6. Blend the sorrel sauce with a hand blender for
    30 seconds to give it an airy, bubbly consistency.

7. Pour about 30 g (1 oz/2 tablespoons) of sauce on
    to each plate, garnish with a few fresh sorrel leaves
    and serve immediately.

BRAISED RABBIT TORTELLINI,
SPRING BROTH, WILD GARLIC

Serves 6 (10 tortellini per person)

There is a lot of work behind this dish, the steps are multiple, but the result is a true concentration of spring, all played out in the delicate and sweet notes of broad beans, peas and rabbit, with the aromatic counterpoint of wild garlic, which grows abundantly in our area, especially in April. You can decide to divide up the work, perhaps preparing the filling in advance and involving friends or family in shelling the broad beans and peas, or filling the ravioli. If the whole process seems like too much, I recommend at least trying the broth; it is the most interesting part, and will still be delicious without the other components. Every spring we found ourselves with a huge pile of pods and, after several experiments in how to use them, we came up with this broth, which captures the elegant flavour of the season and tastes like fresh grass.

Ingredients

For the pasta
200 g (7 oz) '00' flour
50 g (2 oz) semolina flour
3 g (⅛ oz/½ teaspoon) salt
1 small egg (about 40 g/1½ oz)
7 egg yolks (about 140 g/4¾ oz)
10 g (½ oz/2 teaspoons) extra virgin olive oil

For the filling
400 g (14 oz) Rabbit Rillettes (page 190),
    at room temperature
100 g (3½ oz) Parmigiano Reggiano, grated
zest of 1 lemon
1 nutmeg, grated

For the broth
500 g (1 lb 2oz) pea pods, halved diagonally
bunch of mint
4 bay leaves
2 lemons
3 cm (1¼ in) piece of fresh root ginger, sliced
salt

To finish
150 g (5 oz) freshly shelled peas
200 g (7 oz) freshly shelled broad (fava) beans
extra virgin olive oil, salt
wild garlic flowers

Method

1. Make the pasta dough: Mix the flour and semolina flour in the bowl of a stand mixer and add the salt. In a jug, beat together the egg, egg yolks and oil. Slowly add the liquids to the dry ingredients and knead on a medium speed for 7–10 minutes. The dough should be elastic and perfectly combined. Cover with cling film (plastic wrap) and leave to rest for at least 4 hours in the refrigerator.

2. Make the filling: In a large bowl, mix together the rabbit rillettes, Parmigiano, lemon zest and freshly grated nutmeg. Combine until you have a firm mixture and check the flavour (see Chef's Notes). Allow to rest for 2 hours at room temperature.

3. Make the broth: Add half of the pea pods to a blender, along with 750 ml (25 fl oz/3 cups) water. Blend, then transfer to a large saucepan and repeat with the remaining pea pods and another 750 ml (25 fl oz/3 cups) water. You will get a fibrous, green liquid with a distinctly herbaceous smell; no fear, this is perfectly normal. Bring to the boil, then strain through a sieve lined with muslin (cheese cloth). Allow it to drip through without pressure to obtain a clear broth.

4. Pour the resulting liquid into a saucepan over a low heat. Bring up the temperature to 60°C (140°F), then add the mint leaves, bay leaves, lemon peel and ginger. Reduce the heat to very low and leave for 2 hours to infuse gently, but steadily. Strain again and taste, adjusting salt and acidity with a few drops of lemon as needed.

5. Make the tortellini: Roll out the dough with the help of a pasta machine, making it as thin as possible; you need to be able to almost see through it.

6. Once rolled out, cut into 5.5 cm (2¼ in) squares and distribute the filling in small knobs in the centre of each square. Moisten the edges of one of the squares with a little water and fold diagonally into a triangle shape, making sure to tightly encase the filling without leaving air bubbles.

→   Continued on Following Page

7. Now join the two bottom corners together into the classic tortellini shape. Proceed with the other squares and filling until you run out of ingredients (make sure you have 10 tortellini per person).

8. Placed the filled tortellini on a tray, well spaced out and covered with a clean tea towel.

9. Prepare the peas and broad beans: Bring a saucepan of salted water to the boil and blanch the peas and broad beans for 3 minutes. Drain and transfer straight into a bowl of iced water to stop further cooking and maintain the bright green colour.

10. Drain again and peel the broad beans. Place in a small bowl and season with olive oil and salt.

11. Cook and assemble: Cook the tortellini in a pan of boiling salted water for about 3 minutes; taste to check they are cooked.

12. Meanwhile, divide the broad beans and peas between six warm bowls.

13. Drain the tortellini and divide them between the bowls. Cover with the warm broth and finish with a little extra virgin olive oil and wild garlic flowers.

Chef's Notes:

Getting the texture and taste right: If the filling mixture seems too dry (which it may, depending on the firmness of the rabbit), a little beaten egg can help. If it tastes too savoury, you can balance it out by adding some unsalted boiled potato or ricotta.

SEA URCHIN RISOTTO

Serves 6

This risotto was born by chance, as so often happens in the kitchen. After catering an event, we found ourselves with a few leftover sea urchins, an ingredient too precious and rare not to make the most of. In the fridge, there were also some already blanched broad beans and some local gorgonzola cheese. The idea was almost immediate: to combine the iodine note of the sea urchins with the sweetness of the broad beans and the inviting, slightly spicy creaminess of the gorgonzola.

The result is a risotto that is difficult to explain. The combination of ingredients may sound particularly daring, but everything balances well. Rather than there being a single protagonist, the elements play with each other, right up to the last mouthful.

Ingredients

6 large sea urchins
200 g (7 oz) freshly shelled broad (fava) beans
lemon juice, to taste
1.5 litres (51 fl oz/6 cups) Vegetable Broth (page 243)
20 g (3/4 oz) olive oil
320 g (10 ¾ oz) Carnaroli rice
100 g (3½ oz/scant ½ cup) dry white wine
leaves from 2 mint sprigs, finely sliced
120 g (4¼ oz) creamy Gorgonzola
40 g (1½ oz) freshly grated Parmigiano Reggiano
15 g (½ oz) rice vinegar
extra virgin olive oil, salt, ground white pepper

To serve
lemon zest
wild fennel

Method

1. Prepare the sea urchins: To clean the urchins, it is advisable to wear appropriate gloves, especially if you are not familiar with them. Use scissors to cut off the upper ends and drain off the water and any residue and dark membranes.

2. Rinse the urchins in a bowl of cold water, then scoop out the orange pulp using a small teaspoon. Keep the pulp in an airtight container in the refrigerator until ready to use.

3. Cook the broad beans: Bring a saucepan of salted water to the boil and blanch the broad beans for 3 minutes. Drain and transfer straight into a bowl of iced water to stop further cooking and maintain the bright green colour. Drain again and peel to remove the outer skin.

4. Place the broad beans in a small bowl, and season with extra virgin olive oil, salt, a few drops of lemon juice and white pepper.

5. Make the risotto: Pour the broth into a large saucepan and place over a medium heat. Check that it is well salted and keep at a gentle simmer.

6. Heat the olive oil in a medium-sized saucepan over a medium heat. Add the rice and toast for about 4 minutes. Deglaze with the wine, then allow the alcohol to evaporate for 1 minute. Now adding a ladleful of broth; it should just barely cover the rice. Cook, stirring often, and making sure the rice is gently bubbling; it should not be boiling, but neither should the heat be too low. Whenever the broth starts to dry up, add another ladleful. The cooking time will vary depending on the quality of the rice; it can range from 13 to 18 minutes. Taste it often so that you can adjust the seasoning accordingly.

7. When the rice is ready, take the pan off the heat and stir through the broad beans, mint, Gorgonzola and Parmigiano and rice vinegar. Cover the pan with the lid and leave for 2 minutes, then stir vigorously. Add a little broth if it has dried out; it should have a creamy, well-emulsified consistency.

8. Serve: Divide the risotto between six plates, tapping each one lightly on the work surface to spread the rice. Distribute the urchin pulp over the top, and finish with a little lemon zest and fennel.

RICOTTA AND BOTTARGA GNOCCHI, ANCHOVY
BROWN BUTTER, BITTER GREENS

Serves 6

There are many things that have made me fall in love with this region, and ricotta is one of them – especially the kind produced in spring. It is particularly aromatic and fragrant. After winter, the pastures are filled with fresh grass and wild herbs, which gives it a herbaceous note. Here, it is combined with the saline flavours of bottarga and anchovy, then finished with bitter herbs.

Ingredients

For the gnocchi
500 g (1 lb 2oz) fresh ricotta
65 g (2¼ oz) egg yolk
40 g (1½ oz) Parmigiano Reggiano, grated
35 g (1¼ oz) grated bottarga
50 g (2 oz/scant ½ cup) semolina
about 150 g (5 oz/scant ½ cup) '00' flour
    (depending on absorption), plus extra for dusting

For the anchovy brown butter
260 g (9½ oz) Brown Butter (page 233)
25 anchovies
10 sage leaves
2 garlic cloves, sliced

To serve
200 g (7 oz) small wild chicory
lemon juice, to taste
wild flowers, such as marigolds, chamomile or
    wild rocket, preferably bitter and slightly spicy
salt

Method

1. Make the gnocchi: Start by draining the ricotta to remove as much whey as possible. To do this, wrap the ricotta in a muslin (cheese cloth), then place it in a colander set over a bowl. Place something very heavy on top, and leave to drip for at least an hour. It should lose about 20 per cent of its weight. Remove the ricotta from the cloth and weight it; we're aiming to obtain 400 g (14 oz) of dried-out ricotta.

2. Transfer the ricotta to a large bowl. Add the egg yolks, Parmigiano and bottarga and mix to combine.

3. Tip the semolina and half of the '00' flour on to a wooden board. Add the ricotta mixture and knead it into the flour mixture with the help of a metal scraper, gradually adding more flour if the mixture is too wet. Knead just enough to hold the dough together; kneading too much will create gluten, making the dough sticky and elastic.

4. Clean the surface well, then roll the dough into ropes about 2 cm (¾ in) thick. Keeping your hands flat as you roll will ensure a nice regular diameter. Cut each rope into 3 cm (1¼ in) pieces. Place the gnocchi on a floured tray, ensuring they are well spaced out, and keep in the refrigerator until ready to use.

5. Make the butter: Heat the Brown Butter in a saucepan over a medium heat. Add the anchovies, sage leaves and garlic, and cook for 5 minutes. Take off the heat and leave to infuse for 30 minutes, then strain and set aside.

6. Prepare the chicory: Clean the chicory, removing the tough parts and choosing the tender, young leaves. Wash well and dry with paper towels. Bring a saucepan of salted water to the boil and blanch the chicory leaves for 3 minutes. Drain and transfer straight into a bowl of iced water to stop further cooking. Drain again, then pat dry with paper towels.

7. Season with a little of the anchovy butter, a pinch of salt and a few drops of lemon juice.

8. Cook the gnocchi and assemble: Bring a large saucepan of salted water to the boil, then add the gnocchi and cook, stirring occasionally, until they float to the surface. This should take 4 minutes.

9. Put half the warm anchovy brown butter into a warm bowl. Remove the gnocchi from the pan with a slotted spoon and transfer them to this bowl. Move the bowl in circular motions to glaze the gnocchi, adding a little of the cooking water if necessary. They should be glossy and well emulsified.

10. Divide the gnocchi between six warm shallow bowls, taking care to handle them gently. Top with the chicory, arranging it in a natural and graceful way. Finish with a little more brown butter and a few wild flowers, and serve.

SEA BREAM,
SEARED LETTUCE, LARDO

Serves 6

Every year in early spring, we plant many salad varieties, perhaps more than we need. And every year, the time comes when we no longer know what to do with them. When we see our gardener arriving with two huge boxes of salad leaves, we begin to cast worried glances at each other, knowing full well what lies ahead. This dish was born precisely out of this situation, and we decided to experiment with deviating from what we expect a fresh salad to be. We give equal importance to fish and lettuce, applying care and technique to both, overturning the classic concept of main protein and side dish. The lardo adds a touch of silky fattiness that unites the two main elements, guaranteeing both yumminess and flavour.

Ingredients

700 g (1 lb 9 oz) seabream fillet
30 g (2 oz) olive oil
90 g (3¼ oz) thinly sliced lardo
mixture of wild herbs (such as purslane,
    fennel, sorrel and pimpinella)
salt

For the lettuce
3 small butter lettuces
30 g (2 oz) olive oil
2 garlic cloves, peeled
Garlic Citronette (page 234)

For the sauce
60 g (2 oz) Fish Broth (page 241)
50 g (2 oz) Almond Emulsion (page 232)

Method

1. Sear the lettuce: Remove the most damaged outer leaves from each lettuce and trim the bases to remove any darker, tough parts. Halve each one lengthways.

2. Heat the olive oil in a medium-sized frying pan over a medium heat. Add the garlic cloves and gently cook them for 6 minutes until golden and deliciously fragrant. Salt the lettuce halves well and place them cut-side down in the pan, preferably with a weight on top, so that they are pressed into the hot surface of the pan. Cook for 3 minutes, then reduce the heat to low and cook for a further 2 minutes. The lettuce should remain firm and not mushy.

3. Season with the garlic citronette, massage well and keep warm while you prepare the rest of the dish.

4. Make the sauce: Pour the Fish Broth into a small saucepan over a medium heat. As soon as it comes to simmer, take the pan off the heat and add the Almond Emulsion. Stir with a whisk to emulsify. The mixture should be creamy, but not too thick; if necessary, you can add a little water. Adjust the seasoning and keep warm.

5. Cook the fish: Preheat the oven to 160°C fan (320°F/gas 4).

6. Portion the fish into 6 regular fillets, removing any bones. I prefer to use the dorsal side here, which is high and firm, and keep the belly for other uses. Salt each portion of fish well, both on skin and flesh.

7. Heat the oil in a cast-iron pan over a medium-low heat. Add the fish, skin-side down, and cook for 6 minutes until the skin is golden and crispy and you can see an opaque layer on the side, which means the fish is also cooking well. Turn the fish over, then turn off the heat and let it finish cooking in the pan's residual heat. After 2 minutes, transfer to a small tray.

8. Place a slice of lardo on the skin side of each fillet, then transfer to the oven for 1 minute. The lardo will become translucent with the heat.

9. Assemble: Lightly trim the lettuce halves and adjust the seasoning as needed.

10. Take out six warm plates, and pour a little of the sauce into the centre of each one. Place the fish on top and cover gracefully with the salad leaves. Top with the herb mix and serve immediately.

LAMB, MIZUNA, MUSTARD SEEDS

Serves 6

This lamb is the result of careful study by our Manu, who, after several attempts and experiments, has come up with a very accurate and respectful way of preparing lamb that is so different from many classic preparations. Marinating, cooking, smoking and resting make it as fine as a sophisticated cured meat, compacting the lamb but keeping it tender, delicate and complex at the same time. Naturally, the lamb is Michele Varvara's.

Ingredients

1 boneless leg of lamb (about 1–1.2 kg/2 lb 4 oz–2lb 10 oz)
2.5 litres (87 fl oz/10 cups) Brine (page 241)
freshly ground black pepper, sea salt flakes

To serve
70 g (2¼ oz) Meat Jus (page 236)
30 g (1 oz/2 tablespoons) pickled mustard seeds
100 g (3½ oz) mizuna leaves
Garlic Citronette (page 234)

Method

1. Marinate the lamb: Prepare the marinade and leave to cool in a large container. Submerge the leg of lamb in the marinade and make sure it is perfectly covered. Refrigerate for 6 hours.

2. Remove the lamb from the marinade and dry well using paper towels. If possible, leave to dry in the refrigerator, uncovered and placed on a wire rack over a plate, for a few hours or overnight.

3. Cook the lamb: The following day, cook the lamb in a steam oven at 70°C (158°F) for 1 hour 30 minutes, until it reaches 63°C (145°F) at the core – be sure to check this with a thermometer.

4. If you like, you can now sear it in a cast-iron frying pan for 2 minutes over a medium heat, to achieve a colourful, caramelised surface, or you can opt to roast it in a barbecue for 15–20 minutes to add a smoky note. Be careful not to overcook, as the inside is already perfectly done.

5. Leave to rest for 3 hours or until the following day; this serves to compact the meat evenly.

6. Assemble: When you're ready to serve, heat up the jus in a small saucepan over a low heat. Add the pickled mustard seeds and stir to combine.

7. In a bowl, season the mizuna with the Citronette.

8. Slice the lamb into 4 mm (¼ in) slices and arrange on three serving plates. Top with the jus, then add the seasoned mizuna and finish with a grinding of pepper and a good pinch of flaky salt.

PANE E CIOCCOLATO

Serves 6

My childhood breakfast, especially around Easter, was always bread and chocolate. This is a slightly revised formula that I created in my first year here; I wanted to give customers something very comforting, Italian and familiar, true to the original, but with an extra special touch. Here, a rich, silky custard is paired with a slice of Luca's pan brioche, freshly grilled for a crispy texture and very soft inside. It's finished with a drizzle of extra virgin olive oil and salt, which have the mysterious effect of making chocolate even more like itself.

Ingredients

6 thick slices of Olive Oil Pan Brioche (page 239)
extra virgin olive oil, for brushing
sea salt flakes
rosemary flowers

For the chocolate custard
500 g (1 lb 2oz/2 cups) milk
5 g (¼ oz/1 teaspoon) coffee powder
1 tonka bean, grated
75 g (2½ oz) egg yolks (from about 5 eggs)
120 g (4¼ oz/generous ½ cup) sugar
20 g (¾ oz/2 tablespoons) cornflour (cornstarch)
220 g (7¾ oz) dark chocolate (70 per cent cocoa solids)
35 g (1½ oz) butter
2 g (½ teaspoon) salt

Method

1. Make the custard: Heat the milk in a medium saucepan over a medium low heat, stirring often to prevent it from burning at the bottom. Once it reaches a gentle simmer, add the coffee powder and grated tonka bean, then take off the heat and leave to infuse for 15 minutes.

2. In a bowl, mix together the egg yolks, sugar and cornflour with a whisk.

3. Strain the milk through a fine mesh strainer and make sure it's still warm. Gradually add the egg mixture, stirring with a whisk between each addition.

4. Return to a low–medium heat and cook, stirring constantly, until small bubbles appear on the surface. Take it off the heat once more, then add the chocolate and butter, stirring until completely melted. Scrape down the sides of the pan with a spatula to ensure everything is incorporated.

5. Pour the custard into a container and cover with cling film (plastic wrap). Leave to cool, then once it reaches room temperature, transfer to the fridge for 2 hours to chill and stabilise.

6. Assemble: Lightly brush the brioche slices with extra virgin olive oil. Preheat the grill (broiler) to 210°C (410°F), then grill the brioche slices for 5 minutes until golden brown but still soft inside. Leave to cool for a few minutes on a cooling rack.

7. Transfer the chocolate custard into a piping bag fitted with a 1 cm (½ in) nozzle.

8. Cut the brioche slices in half and fill generously with the chocolate custard, piping it in in waves. Finish with a drizzle of olive oil, a pinch of flaky salt and some rosemary flowers. Serve immediately.

ON STRAWBERRIES

The arrival of strawberries marks the return of the tasty and interesting fruit after months of nothing but apples, pears and citrus fruits. Working seasonally means waiting for an ingredient to return to the market, not indulging in the shortcuts of greenhouse products or imports.

Southern Italy, especially Puglia and Basilicata, is known for its abundant cultivation of strawberries. When visiting the market, I try to avoid the eye-catching baskets of huge, perfect strawberries, which have, in all likelihood, been grown with excessive water and under artificial lamps. The strawberries I love to bring into my kitchen are small, imperfect, ranging in colour from red to light pink, characterised by an unmistakable fragrance and firm texture. Even in their unripe stage, they have their own identity: they are fresh, tart, almost crunchy.

We have a small part of the garden dedicated to strawberries. From May to October, it constantly produces small quantities of firm, fragrant and flavourful fruit. When they are available, I don't dare to intervene; I blot them to remove the soil and serve them on a marble tile, at the end of a meal, accompanied by a herbal infusion and madeleines.

If we move away from classic recipes such as fruit tart or jam, the strawberry bears important similarities to the tomato in that it combines with many different ingredients, demonstrating a unique versatility.

If you taste a strawberry and listen only to your palate, sweetness will not dominate, but rather a complex explosion of freshness, fragrance and minerality. For this reason, at Moroseta we enjoy presenting them in unusual ways, highlighting their ability to surprise. That doesn't mean we don't employ them in simpler ways as well – how can anyone resist whipped cream, marinated strawberries and meringues? Or a freshly made jam with brioche bread and salted butter?

STRAWBERRY AND TOMATO

As I explained above, these two ingredients are extremely similar in many respects, which is why they can be combined or alternated very easily, achieving unexpected but absolutely sensible results. Some examples that will convince you: tomato and strawberry gazpacho, strawberry and cherry tomato caprese salad, strawberry and tomato sorbet.

STRAWBERRY AND FRESH CHEESE

Instead of classic whipped cream, I prefer the light acidity and flavour of fresh cheeses, such as ricotta, Robiola or mascarpone. Macerate the strawberries in sugar, flavourings and lemon for at least half an hour first.

STRAWBERRIES AND CHILLI

I think I have very rarely made a strawberry dish that didn't include chilli. The aromatic nature of the strawberry contrasts deliciously with the chilli, which enhances it rather than overpowering it, making it even more interesting and deep.

STRAWBERRY AND PEPPER

Several types of pepper work well with strawberries, above all Timut pepper, which, with its zesty grapefruit aroma, brightens up the strawberry, making it balsamic and very fresh, perfect for pairing with goat's cheese and toasted bread.

STRAWBERRY AND BASIL

The strawberry's affinity with tomatoes makes this combination a must. Try dressing strawberries just as you would a tomato salad, with olive oil, salt, a few drops of red wine vinegar and lots of fresh basil – the result is nothing less than incredible.

STRAWBERRY, BEETROOT AND CHILLI SORBET

Makes 1 kg (2 lb 2 oz)

As soon as strawberry season starts, this sorbet makes a strong comeback on our menu. Once you try the combination of strawberries and chilli, you will you never go back; it seems these two elements were born to be together. The beetroot adds sweetness and that slight earthy touch that adds structure to the whole.

Ingredients

For the syrup
230 g (8 oz) water
155 g (5 oz/generous ⅔ cup) sugar
3 g (⅛ oz) carob seed powder

For the purée
500 g (1 lb 2oz) strawberries, washed and hulled
100 g (3½ oz) beetroot (beets), peeled
    and roughly chopped
30 g (1 oz/2 tablespoons) lemon juice
20 g (¾ oz/4 teaspoons) spicy vinegar
35 g (1¼ oz) Spicy Honey (page 237)
2 g (⅛ oz/scant ¼ teaspoon) salt

Method

1. Make the syrup: Heat the water in a saucepan over a medium heat. Gradually stir in the sugars and carob seed powder. Continue cooking, until the mixture reaches 85°C (185°F), stirring often.

2. Prepare an ice bath by filling a large container or deep tray with iced water.

3. Transfer the syrup into a bowl and cool down quickly by sitting it in the ice bath.

4. Make the fruit purée: In a blender, combine all the purée ingredients and blend until you get a smooth purée.

5. Pass it through a sieve; the beetroot may remain a little sandy in texture.

6. Make the sorbet: Once the syrup is cold, add it to the purée and mix for a few seconds with an immersion blender. Transfer to the refrigerator and leave for 12 hours or overnight.

7. After 12 hours, blend again for a few seconds and then add to your ice cream machine and churn according to the manufacturer's instructions.

STRAWBERRY AND
LAVENDER SHRUB

Makes about 1.5 litres (50 fl oz)

As soon as strawberries are available on our supplier Antonio's list, we start ordering them in copious quantities, using them in every meal, in both savoury and sweet dishes.

When cleaning strawberries, no matter how careful you are, that thin layer of pulp always remains attached to the green stalk. This shrub is largely made using that waste, which you can't really eat, but which nevertheless releases a distinct strawberry scent with herbaceous and fruity notes. These are emphasised by the use of lavender from our garden, which is pruned at precisely the same time.

Ingredients

350 g strawberries (halved if large)
500 g (1 lb 2oz) strawberry hulls
500 g (1 lb 2oz/scant 2¼ cups) sugar
400 ml (13 fl oz/generous 1½ cups) water
40 g (1½ oz) lavender
zest and juice of 2 lemons
300 ml (10 fl oz/1¼ cups) unpasteurised apple cider vinegar

Method

1. In a large saucepan over a medium heat, combine the strawberries, strawberry trimmings, sugar, water, lavender and lemon zest. Bring to the boil, then reduce the heat to low and simmer very gently for 1 hour. If the liquid reduces too much, add a little more water.

2. Transfer into a container and add the lemon juice. Mix well and leave to rest at room temperature for 24 hours.

3. The next day, add the vinegar. Leave to macerate for a couple of days, then strain everything and transfer the resulting liquid into a sterilised glass bottle.

4. This will keep in the fridge for up to 3 months.

ELDERFLOWER VINEGAR

Makes 3 litres (101 fl oz)

I have always loved elderflower, with its delicate, evocative scent, and the beauty of those tiny white lace-like flowers that mark the heart of spring. Sadly, it is not very common in Puglia. I had just about come to terms with this when, after some research, I discovered that Giuseppe, our trusted supplier of fresh cheese and vegetables, has a big elderflower tree on his farm. So, from mid-April onwards each year, I start bombarding him with messages to bring me some flowers. When the flowers from the lower branches run out and he tries to tell me that he cannot retrieve the others, I urge him to get a ladder and pick from the higher branches, trying to convince him that it is of vital importance to seize the moment when it comes to nature, and that if we miss this opportunity, we will have to wait a whole year before we can have any.

Thank you, Giuseppe, for listening to my requests, for allowing me to make this incredible vinegar, and for climbing the ladder, even when you don't feel like it.

Ingredients

250 g (9 oz) elderflowers
3 litres (104 fl oz/12 cups) unpasteurised apple
    cider vinegar
150 g (5 oz/scant ½ cup) honey

Method

1. Sterilise a 3-litre jar with a hermetic seal.

2. If the elderflowers need cleaning, immerse them in a bowl of cold water, but do not wash them under running water, as the pressure of the jet would risk detaching the flowers.

3. Fill the sterilised jar with the elderflowers, fitting in as many as possible but without crushing them.

4. Heat a little of the vinegar in a small saucepan over a medium heat for 5 minutes, then pour it into a large jug. Add the honey and stir to dissolve in the warm vinegar. Add the rest of the vinegar, then pour it into the jar, filling it up to the brim.

5. Close the jar and sterilise.

6. Leave to macerate for at least 6 weeks before using. Once opened, store in the refrigerator. It will keep for about 3 months.

Chef's Notes

Fig Leaf Vinegar: fig leaves can be lightly roasted or left raw. Roasted they will have a more coconut-like aroma, while fresh they will have incredible herbaceous hints. Let infuse at least 2 months before using.

02 SUMMER

Summer is the beating heart of the whole year, when everything is vibrant, dense
and alive. The warm days, the expanses of red earth under the olive trees, the
scent of the scortched countryside, the sound of cicadas at the end of the day.
It is also the season of abundance, of products, colours and flavours. From garden
figs, to fragrant and velvety peaches, to refreshing cucumbers and shiny aubergines.

Our summer menu doesn't have a lot of frills because the raw ingredients are
the protagonists – we just create a few contrasts to highlight their extraordinary
flavours. When you have the great privilege of working with such incredible
ingredients, the main task is discovering how to enhance them. What could be
better than tomatoes still warm from the sun with some freshly baked bread?

COURGETTES,
FIGS, HAZELNUTS

Serves 6

This combination of ingredients is one of our favourites, and we have been using it for a couple of years now, with slight variations. When the late summer figs arrive, firm and very sweet, they provide the perfect contrast to the marked acidity of the marinated courgettes. To top it all off, we add a handful of hazelnuts and our much-loved Almond Emulsion, which give it roundness, fattiness and that ever-needed touch of umami.

You need to plan a little in advance; the courgettes need to rest in the marinade for at least three hours to let themselves go, becoming silky and absorbing all the seasoning.

Ingredients

600 g (1 lb 5 oz) medium-sized yellow courgettes
    (zucchini) (green ones are also fine), cut with a
    mandoline into long ribbons about 3 mm (⅛ in) thick
a few mint sprigs
8 ripe but firm figs
40 g (1½ oz/3¼ tablespoons) caster (superfine) sugar
120 g (4¼ oz) roasted hazelnuts
grated zest of ½ lemon
240 g (8½ oz) Almond Emulsion (page 232)
extra virgin olive oil
Garlic Oil, (page 244) for drizzling
sea salt flakes
timut pepper
wild fennel fronds with flowers, to garnish

For the marinade
240 g (8½ oz/1 cup) apple cider vinegar
150 g (5 oz/scant ¾ cup) olive oil
140 g (4¾ oz/scant ⅔ cup) water
10 g (½ oz/2 teaspoons) salt
1 garlic clove, grated

Method

1. Marinate the courgettes: Combine all the marinade ingredients in a jug. Emulsify by blending with a hand blender for a few seconds, then set aside.

2. In a large Tupperware container (about 30 × 25 × 18 cm / 12 × 10 × 7 in), arrange a layer of the courgette strips, without overlapping them. Season with a pinch of salt, scatter over a few mint leaves, and moisten generously with the marinade. Repeat with a second layer of courgettes, arranging them perpendicularly to the layer below, and seasoning with salt, then topping with mint leaves and marinade. Repeat until all the ingredients are used up, then cover the container with cling film (plastic wrap) and place weights on top to ensure everything is well submerged. Place in the refrigerator for three hours, or overnight.

3. Prepare the figs: Cut each figs into four even wedges and place on a small metal baking tray. Sprinkle over the sugar, then drizzle with oil and scatter over some freshly ground timut pepper. Burn for a few seconds with a blowtorch, until the edges begin to darken and you can smell a nice caramel aroma.

4. Assemble: Coarsely crush the hazelnuts using a pestle and mortar, then tip into a small bowl. Season with a drizzle of garlic oil and pinch of salt, then scatter over the lemon zest. Mix well and taste; they should be delicious.

5. To serve, divide the marinated courgette ribbons between six plates. Fill a piping bag with the Almond Emulsion and pipe it in among the ribbons in small, regular dollops. Top with the figs, then scatter over the seasoned hazelnuts. Finish with the wild fennel and its flowers, along with a pinch of salt and a drizzle of extra virgin olive oil.

Serves 6

I have never liked the idea of a signature dish; whenever I was asked what mine was, I always replied that I didn't have one; the idea of repeating the same thing over and over horrified me.

However, I believe that if I asked our returning guests the same thing, they would answer, without a doubt, 'Gazpacho!' It has been a recurring item on our tasting menus since the very beginning, served in all possible variations and combinations from the early days of May until the first days of October. It is a dish I like to serve at the start of a meal, a preamble to the tasting menu; it is fresh, light and 100 per cent plant-based, and can pack an unexpected level of complexity.

In this case, the gazpacho, unlike the Andalusian recipe, is made with roasted vegetables, emphasising their round, caramel-like flavour as opposed to the pungent freshness of the red wine vinegar. It's more a method than a recipe; once you get into the gazpacho game, the possibilities are endless.

Ingredients

50 g (2 oz) finely sliced red onion
50 g (2 oz/3 tablespoons) red wine vinegar
50 g (2 oz/3 tablespoons) water
15 basil leaves
45 g (1¾ oz/3 tablespoons) extra virgin olive oil
5 g (¼ oz/1 teaspoon) ground cumin
salt, freshly ground black pepper

For the roasted vegetables
400 g (14 oz) (bell) peppers, cut into bite-sized pieces
700 g (1 lb 9 oz)g San Marzano tomatoes, quartered
250 g (9 oz) carrots, peeled and cut into rounds
350 g (11 oz) apricots, stoned and halved
50 g (2 oz/3 tablespoons) extra virgin olive oil
10 g (½ oz/2 teaspoons) salt

To serve
100 g (3½ oz) raspberries
60 g (2 oz) currants
pinch of sumac
sorrel, or another aromatic herb of your choice
Bay Leaf Oil (page 245)

Method

1. Roast the vegetables: Preheat the oven to 200°C fan (400°F/gas 7).

2. Combine the peppers, tomatoes, carrots and apricots in a large bowl. Drizzle with the oil, then season with the salt and some freshly ground black pepper, and toss well. Tip into a large baking tray and spread out; they should not be packed too tightly together, otherwise they will steam instead of roasting and caramelising.

3. Roast for 25–30 minutes, stirring halfway through. The vegetables should be well cooked, soft and golden brown.

4. While the vegetables are cooking, place the onion slices in a small bowl and cover with the vinegar and water. Leave to marinate for half an hour.

5. Blend: Tip the roasted vegetables into a blender, along with the onion and its marinating liquid. Add the basil leaves and 45 g (1¾ oz/3 tablespoons) oil, then blend for 2 minutes at high speed.

6. The consistency should be quite loose. Add water until the desired texture is reached. You may need to adjust the salt and vinegar, depending on how much water you have added.

7. Transfer the gazpacho to a container, cover with cling film (plastic wrap) and allow to cool completely for 3–4 hours.

8. Assemble: Serve in individual bowls, allowing a generous ladleful per person. Garnish the top with raspberries, currants, a pinch of sumac, sorrel or the herb of your choice and a few drops of bay leaf oil.

Chef's Notes

Let it rest: Personally, I think this soup tastes even better the next day; the flavours get to know each other and really develop. You can store it in the refrigerator for up to three days.

FLAT PEACH, CUCUMBER, MOZZARELLA

Serves 6

We are blessed with fresh dairy products every day, delivered by our cheesemaker Giuseppe at the peak of their expression of texture and taste. This dish is all about our beloved local *fiordilatte* mozzarella in all its sensual milkiness. It has a firm structure and a complex balance between savouriness and sweetness; it's honestly hard to resist.

This dish is one of our classic summer lunches, when the only rule is 'Choose the best ingredients you have available, and season them well.' More than a recipe, it is an invitation to experiment with different elements, creating new contrasts of sweetness and acidity around mozzarella. (To be honest, it's nothing more than a variation of a caprese salad, but that didn't sound very flattering!)

Ingredients

3 white tabacchiere peaches
2 medium-sized cucumbers
800 g (1 lb 12 oz) Apulian fiordilatte mozzarella,
    as fresh as possible
purple and lemon basil leaves
extra virgin olive oil, salt flakes

For the marinade
10 g (½ oz/2 teaspoons) lemon juice
15 g (½ oz/1 tablespoon) rice vinegar
10 g (½ oz/2 teaspoons) Garlic Oil (page 244)
15 g (½ oz) Spicy Honey (page 237)
2 g (1/8 oz) chilli flakes
30 g (1 oz/2 tablespoons) extra virgin olive oil

Method

1. Marinate the peaches: In a bowl, combine all the ingredients for the marinade and emulsify with a whisk.

2. Wash and peel the peaches; white peaches can usually be peeled very easily. Cut each fruit into 6 even segments and arrange in a shallow bowl, then pour over the marinade. Cover and place in the refrigerator for half an hour.

3. Assemble: In the meantime, use a mandoline to slice the cucumbers into slices of about 3 mm (1/8 in). Set aside in a bowl of iced water to keep crispy. When you're ready to serve, drain the cucumber and pat it dry with paper towels.

4. I like to tear the mozzarella with my hands to highlight its stringy texture; the pieces should not be too small, otherwise the mozzarella will lose a lot of milk.

5. To assemble, arrange the peaches, cucumber and mozzarella in bowls, without overlapping them too much. Drizzle with extra virgin olive oil and salt flakes, and scatter over plenty of basil leaves just before serving.

6. This is a dish that is at its best if eaten quickly; everything must be fresh with the right texture and seasoned brightly.

WHITE TURNIP, NECTARINE, GREEN TOMATO AGUACHILE

Serves 6

Laura came up with this condiment somewhat by accident. She'd been asked to create some marinated peaches, a sweet-and-sour fruit chop-chop sauce to go with barbecued shellfish, something reminiscent of the combination of flavours found in a Thai green papaya salad.

Laura's marinated peaches were delicious, but the marinating liquid that was created after a few hours of resting in the refrigerator was absolutely incredible, an explosion of acidity and mouthwatering complexity. It immediately became a constant element of our summer menus, and we paired it with many different ingredients. It works wonderfully on crudo, but in my opinion it is with vegetables that it gives the most surprising results, especially here, with the silky sweetness of white turnip.

Thank you, Laura, for this recipe and also for your patience, happily dicing vegetables all summer long.

Ingredients

3 medium-sized white turnips
1 firm nectarine
2 green tomatoes
purslane or mint flowers (or other aromatic
    herbs of your choice)
Garlic Oil (page 244)
chilli oil, extra virgin olive oil, salt, to serve

For the aguachile sauce
1 fairly ripe nectarine, chopped into small cubes
2 cornaletti chillies, finely chopped (see Chef's Notes)
20 g (¾ oz) red onion, finely chopped
½ garlic clove, grated
20 g (¾ oz/4 teaspoons) lemon juice
15 g (½ oz/1 tablespoon) brown sugar
50 g (2 oz/3 tablespoons) rice vinegar
40 g (1½ oz/2½ tablespoons) fish sauce
2 g (⅛ oz) Korean chilli flakes

Method

1. Prepare the aguachile: Combine all the aguachile sauce ingredients in a container and mix well. Cover with a lid and place in the refrigerator for 3 hours.

2. Prepare the vegetables: In the meantime, steam the white turnips over a medium heat for about 20–25 minutes. The cooking time can vary, so check with a skewer; they should be cooked but still firm. Once ready, rub them with your hands or some paper towel to remove the skin. Allow to cool.

3. Chop the turnips into 5 mm (¼ in) cubes, then do the same with the nectarine and green tomatoes, trying to keep them the same size. Place in a container and refrigerate until ready to use. At the same time, chill six shallow bowls for serving later.

4. Strain the aguachile sauce: After 3 hours, strain the aguachile with a fine-mesh sieve (keep the marinated vegetables aside).

5. Taste the strained liquid and adjust the salt, sweetness and acidity as needed. Bear in mind that it is not a broth but a condiment, so it is normal for it to be rather strong. Transfer the liquid into a squeezing bottle and refrigerate until ready to use.

6. Assemble: Tip the turnips, nectarines and green tomatoes into a large bowl and season lightly with garlic oil, olive oil, a pinch of salt and a generous spoonful of the reserved marinated vegetables.

7. Arrange the vegetables in the chilled serving bowls, then pour a thin layer of the aguachile sauce into each bowl. Finish with the fresh herbs and a few drops of chilli oil. Let the ingredients get to know each other for a few minutes, then serve.

Chef's Notes

Vegetable variations: The nectarines, turnips and green tomatoes can be replaced with seasonal fruits and vegetables. We have made this recipe with unripe strawberries, cantaloupe, watermelon, cucumber and celery, always with good results.

TOMATO TOAST

<u>Serves 6</u>

This is definitely one of my absolute favourite things'
I could live on *pane e pomodoro* and never get tired
of it. Over the years, we have explored this theme
in different ways, overlapping, breaking down and
discovering the many possibilities contained within
these humble yet divine ingredients.

This is not the definitive version, just the one we
enjoyed the most this past summer, served mostly
for breakfast. The base is a soft and voluptuous pan
brioche made with extra virgin olive oil. It was created
by Luca, who responded positively to my request for
something fluffy and light to use at breakfast, playing
with local ingredients. After being toasted, the bread
meets a generous layer of roasted tomato paste that
not only provides a boost of natural umami, but also
works as a glue for the fresh tomato slices that are
placed on top, therefore avoiding that annoying but
frequent experience of tomatoes falling ruinously
apart just as you are about to bite into a bruschetta.

This essential version celebrates just two key elements,
but it can be enriched in the most diverse ways.

<u>Ingredients</u>

For the toast
6 slices of Olive Oil Pan Brioche (page 239),
    about 2.5 cm (1 in) thick
300 g (10½ oz) Roasted Tomato Paste (see below)
6 large tomatoes, preferably Costoluto or
    Cuore di Bue
1 garlic clove
fresh herbs of your choice, to garnish
extra virgin olive oil, salt flakes, freshly ground
    black pepper, to serve

For the roasted tomato paste
(makes 500 g/1 lb 2 oz)
2 kg (4 lb 8 oz) small mixed tomatoes
sugar or honey, to taste (optional)

Method

1. Make the roasted tomato paste: Preheat the
   oven to 160°C fan (320°F/gas 4) and line one or
   two baking trays with baking parchment.

2. Wash all the tomatoes for the tomato paste, then
   cut them in half, trying to keep a fairly consistent
   size. Put them into a large bowl and season with
   olive oil, salt and pepper. The seasoning should not
   be too generous, as the tomatoes will dehydrate
   in the oven and lose most of their volume, thus
   concentrating all the flavours.

3. Arrange on the prepared baking tray(s), ensuring
   they aren't crowded too close together, and roast
   for 1 hour, stirring every 20 minutes, making sure
   each one is well caramelised and roasted.

4. Once ready, remove from the oven and let them cool
   for at least half an hour, then finely chop. Tip the
   resulting tomato paste into a large container and
   mix well. Taste and adjust the seasoning if required.

5. Toast and assemble: Increase the oven temperature
   to 220°C (430°F/gas 9).

6. Place the bread slices on a wire rack and toast them
   in the oven for about 6 minutes, until both sides are
   golden brown and fragrant.

7. Once ready, lightly rub one side of each slice of
   toasted bread with the garlic clove to gently infuse
   with its aroma. Spread a generous layer of tomato
   paste on each slice, about 50 g (2 oz) each.

8. Slice the tomatoes into thick slices and arrange
   them on the toasted bread, overlapping slightly.
   Garnish with the fresh herbs and season generously
   with oil, salt flakes and pepper. Serve immediately.

Chef's Notes

Variations on the theme: This tomato-and-bread
base lends itself to myriad additions: fresh cheese, such
as shredded mozzarella or indulgent burrata, anchovies,
for an umami-on-umami overlay, fried or soft-boiled eggs,
or a few slices of prosciutto crudo or capocollo.

ON TOMATOES

My love affair with the tomato began at a young age, long before I decided to dedicate myself to cooking. I have vivid memories of wonderful bruschetta meticulously prepared by my mother during summer holidays: ripe tomatoes cut with precision and seasoned with oil, salt and pepper; bread well toasted and gently rubbed with just enough garlic to complement but not cover up the tomato flavour.

Another powerful memory: spaghetti, served with fresh sauce that had been puréed in a small homemade tomato press at our seaside home, freshly scented with basil broken up with our fingers, and topped with a hint of Parmesan to finish. That scent and intensity is still my standard of perfection in the matter.

If I am asked about my favourite ingredient, the answer is always the same, at least as far as summer is concerned: I adore and worship his majesty the tomato. Specifically, my weakness is tomatoes that are generous in size, ribbed, opulent and rich. Sliced and seasoned generously, they give me unparalleled satisfaction.

Every year, I start observing the market stalls in mid-May and early June, impatiently wandering around, looking for the first to arrive. From the sharp acidity and crunchiness of the Marinda tomatoes to the explosions of sweetness and fleshiness of the August tomato, I love them in all its shades and sizes.

In this, Puglia is truly unbeatable; the unbridled amount of sunshine and an explosive terroir give absolutely unique tomatoes. I have the good fortune to work with an enlightened farmer, Antonio, who not only respects his land and works to keep it healthy and intact, but also devotes much of his time to researching ancient and local seeds. Over the years, we have planted every type of cultivar in the Moroseta garden, discovering exciting flavours and colours that have always found a prominent place in our tasting menus.

TOMATO AND CINNAMON

Cinnamon brings warm, deep nuance to the bright acidity of
tomato, especially when it comes to sauce. We have, for years, made
meatballs spiced with sultanas, citrus zest and mint, which, after
being fried are tossed in a classic tomato sauce, flavoured with a
pinch of cinnamon. We like them so much that they are now part of
the starters served at our weddings.

TOMATO AND VANILLA

The sweetness of vanilla balances the acidity of tomato well,
but be careful to use it in moderation, as it can easily become
overpowering. Fresh tomato pulp can be seasoned with a hint of
vanilla to make a fresh dressing to go with shellfish, such as
langoustines, whose butteriness will pair well with the freshness
of the tomato and the soft vanilla note. Alternatively, you can
make a smoked tomato and vanilla chutney to serve with soft
goat's cheeses and crunchy bread.

TOMATO AND ANCHOVY

This is the combination that makes my heart beat faster: an explosion
of umami, savouriness and acidity. The perfect approach is to make
a Spanish pan con tomate, topped with two anchovy fillets and a
drizzle of extra virgin olive oil.

TOMATO AND MELON

The sweetness of ripe melon mellows out the acidity of the tomato
and amplifies its bouquet of aromas. High-quality tomatoes and
cantaloupe melon, dressed with olive oil and a few drops of wine
vinegar, flavoured with chilli and mint and basil leaves, topped with
some shredded buffalo mozzarella, can be something extraordinary.

AUBERGINES, BLACK GARLIC, SUMMER HERBS

Serves 6

The natural meatiness of aubergines (eggplants) makes them unique and extremely versatile, but at the same time, they hide some traps: the cooking time, the tendency towards unpleasant bitterness, the abundance of seeds (especially in the old varieties we use in our kitchen), and the not particularly satisfying greyish-brown colour they turn once cooked.

After experimenting with aubergines in sauces, terrines, tartares and fillings without any particular success, we decided to return to their original form, handling them with more respect and care. This is the result.

The co-star is black garlic, used as a silky emulsion that envelops and softens the edginess of the aubergine. The final touch is a garden of fresh herbs, simply seasoned with a few drops of lemon, making each bite vibrant and unique.

Ingredients

For the aubergine
6 small/medium-sized aubergines (eggplants)
40 g (1½ oz) Carpione Vinegar (page 244)
    (see Chef's Notes)
25 g (1 oz) Soy Sauce and Wine Glaze (page 237)
extra virgin olive oil
sea salt flakes

For the black garlic emulsion
140 g (4¾ oz) peeled black garlic
½ garlic clove
40 g (1½ oz) anchovies
40 g (1½ oz/2½ tablespoons) lemon juice
100 g (3½ oz/scant ½ cup) grape seed oil
20 g (¾ oz/1 tablespoon) honey
10 g (½ oz/2 teaspoons) rice vinegar
35 g (1¼ oz) Parmesan
10 g (½ oz/2 teaspoons) water

To serve
large handful of mixed herbs, such as purslane,
    Greek basil, mint and fennel
a few drops of lemon juice

Method

1. Prepare the aubergines: Wash and dry the aubergines, then cut them in half lengthways, keeping the stalk intact; this will also ensure that they do not flatten too much during cooking.

2. Score each half with criss-crossing diagonal cuts about 5 mm (¼ in) apart, taking care not to push the blade all the way through. Place the aubergine halves on a baking tray, cut-sides up, and season generously with salt, massaging it in to allow the grains of salt to penetrate the cuts. Leave to rest for half an hour to an hour at room temperature.

3. Prepare the black garlic emulsion: Place all the ingredients for the black garlic emulsion in a blender and blend for a couple of minutes at maximum power. Scrape down the sides of the blender with a spatula and blend for a few seconds more, making sure everything is well combined. The result should be shiny, elastic and smooth. Transfer to a squeezing bottle and keep in the refrigerator until ready to use.

4. Bake and glaze the aubergines: Preheat the oven to 210°C (410°F/gas 7).

5. The salt will have drawn liquid out of the aubergines. Pat them well with a clean cloth or paper towel to dry. You can also try squeezing them gently; they will release a lot of water. Once ready, drizzle with oil and return to the baking tray, cut-sides up. Bake for 25–30 minutes until they are nicely coloured and cooked. Transfer to a wire rack and cool completely.

6. In a small bowl, mix together the Carpione Vinegar and glaze. Brush the aubergines well with this, then cover with cling film (plastic wrap) and transfer to the refrigerator for at least 1 hour to rest.

7. Assemble: After resting, arrange the aubergines on a plate. Pipe thin lines of the black garlic emulsion on to each aubergine, adding 10 g (½ oz) to each half.

8. In a large bowl, combine your chosen mixed herbs with the lemon juice and some extra virgin olive oil.

9. Arrange the herbs on top of each aubergine, until they are completely covered. Serve immediately.

MOROSETA

CUTTLEFISH 'TAGLIATELLA',
ALMOND, MISO, WILD FENNEL

Serves 6

Serving cuttlefish raw may seem like an extreme idea, a witchcraft invented by some chef eager to impress, but in Puglia, it is a traditional seafood dish, served without any seasoning (don't you dare ask for lemon). Cut into long, opalescent ribbons, it goes by the characteristic name of '*tagliatella*'. Our version has nothing traditional about it except the classic shape, but I can assure you that it has convinced even the most sceptical of sceptics. The other elements involved are a kind of mayonnaise made of almonds and white miso, along with lemon and wild fennel (my absolute favourite herb), for a play on delicacy that provides an elegant start a summer meal.

Ingredients

For the tagliatella
6 small fresh cuttlefish (about 650 g/1 lb 7 oz)
2 cornaletti chillies, finely sliced
15 g (½ oz/1 tablespoon) rice vinegar
pinch of caster (superfine) sugar
zest of 1 lemon

To serve
60 g (2 oz) Almond Emulsion (page 232)
wild fennel flowers and fronds, to serve
extra virgin olive oil
Garlic Oil (page 244), to serve
salt flakes, timut pepper, to serve

This may seem like a very small amount, but the flavour and texture of raw cuttlefish are very special, and a generous portion might be too much, especially for those who are not used to it.

4. Transfer the cuttlefish ribbons into a container and refrigerate until ready to use.

5. Marinate the chillies: Place the green chillies in a small bowl and season with the rice vinegar and sugar. Mix well and leave to marinate for at least 10 minutes.

6. Place six serving dishes and a mixing bowl in the refrigerator to chill at least 30 minutes before serving.

7. Assemble: Place the cuttlefish in the cold mixing bowl, and season with a few drops of garlic oil and some salt and timut pepper. Grate over the lemon zest. Massage for a few seconds and taste, adjusting the seasoning as needed.

8. Divide the cuttlefish between chilled plates, arranging the ribbons in a pleasing way.

9. Fill a piping bag with the Almond Emulsion and pipe a little of it on to on each plate, making small dots between the cuttlefish ribbons (you'll need about 5 g/¼ oz of emulsion per plate). Garnish with the marinated chilli slices and wild fennel flowers and fronds. Finish with a few drops of olive oil and a pinch of salt flakes, then serve.

Method

1. Prepare the cuttlefish: Clean the cuttlefish carefully (I recommend using gloves, some ink may escape). The tentacles can be kept for other uses; you only need the clean, skinless tubes.

2. Pat them well with paper, then cut one side of each tube so that they open completely and lie flat.

3. Starting from the larger side, slice into thin strips or ribbons, about 3 mm (⅛ in) thick. We will need about 35 g (1¼ oz) of cuttlefish ribbons per portion.

Chef's Notes

Cuttlefish: If you cannot find small cuttlefish, you can also opt for a larger one. If the tube is quite thick, it is advisable, once cleaned, to freeze it for a few hours. It will be more tender and easier to slice thinly.

Raw: If the idea of raw cuttlefish still leaves you in doubt, you can opt to marinate it in lemon juice, which will make it lose some of its slimy texture and gently cook the fish. Alternatively, you can blanch it for a few seconds in boiling water; in this case, you should increase the quantity to 60 g (2 oz) per person.

RAVIOLO 'PANE E POMDORO'
IN TOMATO BROTH

Serves 6

How obsessed can you be with tomatoes? This ingredient offers so many nuances that we just can't put an end to our experimentations. One of the many wonderful things about tomatoes is their natural concentration of free glutamic acid, simply known as the 'umami' element, which increases even more when tomatoes are ripe and cooked.

These ravioli are filled with a concentrated, slow-cooked tomato sauce, which is thickened with stale bread and then further lightly dehydrated in the oven to achieve a complete caramelisation of the natural sugars and an outstanding, mouthwatering result. To counteract this extreme concentration, we pair it with a clear, crystalline broth, the essence of the tomato deprived of its structure, to embrace and elevate the ravioli.

I'll be honest, It is a long and quite laborious process – from start to finish, it takes more than a day – but it is an experience worth having. It allows you to get into the guts of this magical ingredient, and understand it intimately. To be served lukewarm on a summer evening, and enjoyed in silence.

Ingredients

For the pasta
200 g (7 oz/scant 1⅔ cups) '00' flour
50 g (2 oz/scant ½ cup) semolina flour
1 small egg (about 40 g/1½ oz)
7 egg yolks (about 140 g/4¾ oz)
10 g (½ oz/2 teaspoons) extra virgin olive oil,
    plus extra to serve
3 g (1/8 oz/½ teaspoon) salt

For the filling
80 g (3 oz/⅓ cup) olive oil
225 g (8 oz) crustless stale bread, cubed
350 g (11 oz) Manu's Tomato Sauce (page 129)
salt

For the broth
2 g (4 lb 8 oz) mixed tomatoes, washed and
    roughly chopped
bunch of aromatic herbs, such as basil, mint,
    or bay leaves
zest of 2 lemons

Method

1. Make the pasta dough: Make the pasta dough following the directions on page 51. Cover with cling film (plastic wrap) and chill for 4 hours.

2. Make the filling: Preheat the oven to 170°C fan (340°F/gas 5).

3. In a bowl, drizzle the oil over the bread cubes and season with a pinch of salt. Toss to combine, then spread out on a baking tray and toast in the oven for 10 minutes until lightly golden.

4. Heat the tomato sauce in a large saucepan over a medium heat. Add the bread and cook for 5 minutes, stirring well. At this stage, it might not look the best, but that's totally normal. Transfer to a container and leave in the refrigerator for 12 hours to rehydrate.

5. The next day, preheat the oven to 100°C fan (210°F/gas ½) and line a baking tray with baking parchment. Transfer the tomato mixture to a blender and blend until it is quite creamy, but not completely smooth; it is important to leave some texture. Spread the resulting filling on the prepared tray and place in the oven for 1 hour, stirring every 15 minutes so that a crust does not form on the surface.

6. Allow to cool, then taste and adjust the salt as needed. Make sure there are no lumps, then mix well and transfer into a piping bag.

7. Make the ravioli: Roll out the dough into sheets using a pasta machine, or very thinly by hand.

8. Pipe small quantities of the filling (about 8 g/¼ oz each) on to one of the pasta sheets, spacing them well apart. Brush the pasta sheet with a little water between the dollops of filling, then lay another sheet of dough on top. Press with your fingers around the dollops of filling, so that the dough is sealed and any air escapes. Cut out the ravioli with a round cutter.

9. Place on a tray covered with a clean tea towel and set aside.

→   Continued on Following Page

10. **For the broth:** In a blender, blend the tomatoes well until you have a fine liquid pulp is obtained. Transfer this to a medium-sized saucepan and bring to the boil.

11. Allow to boil for 2 minutes, then turn off the heat. The pulp will have concentrated on the surface.

12. Strain the mixture into a clean bowl through a sieve lined with muslin (cheesecloth), letting it drip to obtain a transparent broth.

13. Heat the resulting broth slightly, to a maximum of 60°C (140°F). And add the herbs and lemon zest. Cover with a lid and take off the heat, then leave to infuse for 20 minutes. Strain once more and set aside.

14. **Cook the ravioli and serve:** Bring a large saucepan of salted water to the boil. Add the ravioli and cook for about 4 minutes. Drain using a slotted spoon, then divide the ravioli between 6 bowls.

15. Pour a small ladleful of warm tomato broth into each bowl and finish with a few drops of olive oil.

Chef's Notes

Broth: This broth is absolutely worth trying, regardless of the ravioli. We often serve it pure; a small cup of tomato broth is a great way to start a meal.

BROAD BEAN DUMPLINGS, PEPPER SAUCE

Serves 6

This is one of those dishes whose birth, development and final form I find hard to explain. It is the result of an unconscious conversation where a distinctly Asian-inspired dish moves and marries some of our local ingredients, such as broad beans, garlic and peppers, resulting in something totally different. It sounds nonsensical, but it makes a lot of sense when you eat it. The dumpling dough is made only of flour and cream, a recipe kindly gifted by our friend and chef Alessandro Esposito. It becomes a transparent, elastic envelope with that typical slightly chewy finish: absolutely irresistible. It requires work and a little patience in learning how to handle it, but above all, the right climatic conditions. We tried to make about 400 of these dumplings on one of the hottest and most humid days in history. After that I would recommend cooking this on a cool, breezy day.

Ingredients

For the dough
330 g (11 oz/2⅔ cup) plain (all-purpose) flour
215 g (7½ oz/scant 1 cup) cream
rice flour, for dusting

For the filling
300 g (10½ oz) Broad Bean Hummus (page 233)
60 g (2 oz/generous ½ cup) almond flour
2 Confit Garlic Gloves (page 244), crushed

For the pepper sauce
3 kg (6 lb 8 oz) (bell) peppers, coarsely chopped
2 litres (40 fl oz/8 cups) water
150 g (5 oz/generous ⅔ cup) sugar
325 g (11 ½ oz/1⅓ cups) white wine
45 g (1¾ oz) sage
10 g (½ oz/2 teaspoons) salt
55 g (2 oz) shoyu soy sauce
180 g (6 ½ oz/¾ cup) apple cider vinegar

To serve
'Nduja Oil (page 244)
fresh oregano leaves
Spicy Vinegar (page 245)

Method

1. Make the dough: Add the flour and cream to a stand mixer and mix for 5 minutes at a medium speed, until you have a smooth, elastic dough. Cover and leave to rest for 2 hours.

2. Make the filling: In a bowl, combine the Broad Bean Hummus with the almond flour and crushed confit garlic. Leave to rest for 6 hours, so that the almond flour rehydrates. The amount of almond flour you'll need depends on the moisture content of the purée; you can add a little more flour it if it is still too soft after resting.

3. Make the sauce: In a blender, blend the peppers with the water. You'll need to do this in two batches. Tip the resulting mixture into a large saucepan and bring to the boil. Let it boil for 2 minutes, then take off the heat. The pulp will concentrate on the surface.

4. Strain the mixture into a clean bowl through a sieve lined with muslin (cheesecloth) without applying pressure, to obtain a transparent broth.

5. Make a blond caramel in a medium-sized saucepan with the sugar.

6. Measure 3 litres (101 fl oz/1½ cups) of the broth into a saucepan, off the heat. Add the broth and wine to the caramel. Return to the heat and add the other ingredients. Reduce over a low–medium heat for 2 hours. Taste and adjust the seasoning, then cool.

7. Make the dumplings: Thinly roll out the dough using a pasta machine or very thinly by hand, adding rice flour if sticky. Cut it into 8 cm (3½ in) circles.

8. Place a small amount of filling on each circle, then moisten the edges and fold the dough over itself to create a half-moon shape. Place on a tray covered with a tea towel while you make the rest.

9. Cook and assemble: Bring a large pan of salted water to the boil. Add the dumplings and cook for about 2 minutes. Drain using a slotted spoon, and divide the dumplings between six bowls. Pour a ladleful of broth into each bowl, and finish with a few drops of 'nduja oil, spicy vinegar and oregano leaves.

Serves 6

Yes, that's right: more tomato. I would be lying if I didn't include this many tomato dishes in the summer chapter. I decided to be as sincere as possible in these pages; so, take this long sequence of tomato-centred creations as an act of intellectual honesty.

In the Italian collective imagination, *risotto al pomodoro* is a rather sad dish, summoning up childish memories and disliked by many. We have therefore taken up the challenge and tried to make it complex and enjoyable by layering different elements, such as *bagnacaoda*, smoked tomato powder, preserved tomatoes and the ever-present fresh lemon zest.

A note: in this case, we decided not to emulsify with butter and Parmesan cheese at the end of cooking, as the tomato sauce is already so full of umami that it does not need it, especially if you decide to add extra elements on top (if not, I recommend a light *mantecatura*).

Ingredients

For the risotto
1 litre (34 fl oz/4 cups) Vegetable Broth (page 243)
350 g (11 oz) Manu's Tomato Sauce (page 129)
250 g (9 oz) Carnaroli rice
50 g (2 oz) olive oil
60 g (2 oz/¼ cup) white wine
zest of 1 lemon
65 g (2¼ oz) Garlic Emulsion (page 234)
extra virgin olive oil, salt, freshly ground black pepper

To serve
smoked tomato powder (optional)
fresh herbs of your choice

Method

1. In a large saucepan, heat the broth over a medium heat. Make sure it is well salted and keep at a gentle simmer. In a separate saucepan over a low-medium heat, heat the tomato sauce.

2. Meanwhile, in a medium-sized saucepan over a medium heat, toast the rice with the oil for about 4 minutes.

3. Deglaze with the wine and allow the alcohol to evaporate for 1 minute, then start cooking by adding a ladleful of broth; it should just barely cover the rice. Cook, stirring often and making sure the rice always has a few bubbles. It should not be boiling, but neither should it be too still. Once the broth has been absorbed, add another ladleful.

4. After the first 7 minutes, start adding the warm tomato sauce, adding it in three batches times, always alternating a ladleful of broth. The cooking time will vary depending on the quality of the rice; it can range from 13 to 18 minutes. The important thing is to taste it often, so that you can adjust accordingly. In this case, we like it cooked more al dente: it goes well with the roundness of the tomato.

5. When you're happy with the risotto, turn off the heat and leave to rest for 2 minutes, covered. Then add the lemon zest, a drizzle of olive oil and a grinding of black pepper, and stir vigorously (you might need a little more broth if it has dried out during the resting time; you want a creamy consistency).

6. Divide the risotto between plates, tapping each plate on the counter to flatten the rice. Drizzle the garlic cream over the top, then dust with tomato powder (if using) and finish with the herbs.

Chef's Notes

Smoked tomato powder: making tomato broth often, we constantly have leftover pulp. In order not to waste it, we got into the habit of drying it to make a powder. We spread the pulp on as many baking trays as possible, so that we have a thin layer, and it gets dried in a low oven until completely dry and caramelized. We then smoke them for about 20 minutes and blend to a powder.

OCTOPUS, PERCOCA, GUANCIALE KUSHIYAKI

Makes 12 small skewers

For about a year now, we have been obsessed with skewers – technically called *kushiyaki*, to adopt a cool contemporary cuisine term. There is something irresistible about the creative juxtaposition of barbecued elements on an iron skewer. Cooking and eating in this manner encompasses something ancestral: the smell of the embers, the act of pulling off the pieces and bringing them to the mouth, still hot and steaming.

Here, we combine octopus, the quintessential symbol of Puglia summer food, with guanciale and percoca. These three elements balance each other in a dynamic interplay of succulence, fat and acidity. When cooking, you must make sure that each side is caramelised and crispy, concealing a juicy and tender interior. Before serving, we glaze the skewers with a peach reduction that makes them deliciously sticky and allows us to cover them with chives, toasted sesame and chilli flakes – not compulsory, but definitely recommended.

Ingredients

For the skewers
1.2 kg (2 lb 10 oz) octopus
300 g (10½ oz) sliced guanciale
    (36 thin slices in total)
2 large percoche

For the peach glaze
(makes 300 g/10½ oz)
60 g (2 oz/¼ cup) cane sugar
1 kg (2 lb 4 oz) yellow peaches, stoned and sliced
1 kg (2 lb 4 oz/4 cups) wine
5 g (¼ oz/1 teaspoon) salt
40 g (1½ oz) shoyu
15 g (½ oz) sage leaves
1 fresh chilli

To serve
salt flakes
hot sauce
fresh chives
toasted sesame seeds

Method

1. **Make the glaze:** In a medium saucepan over a low heat, make a blond caramel with the sugar. Add the wine (it will splash a little; this is normal), followed by the sliced peaches and the rest of the ingredients.

2. Reduce the heat to low–medium and cook for 1 hour 20 minutes until the mixture has a thick, syrupy consistency. Strain through a sieve and keep chilled.

3. **Cook the octopus:** Steam the octopus over a low heat for 30–40 minutes. Check the consistency with a skewer at the thickest part, where the tentacles join the head. It should slide in easily. Be careful not to over-cook it. Allow to cool completely.

4. **Assemble and cook:** Stone the percoche and slice into regular slices, 1cm (½ in) thick.

5. Separate the octopus tentacles and slice them diagonally so that you have thin slices 4 cm (1½ in) long. You will need 36 slices in total.

6. Bunch up each slice of guanciale, so that it creates a wavy shape similar in size to the octopus and peach.

7. Build the skewers by alternating the elements. Percoca tends to soften during cooking, so it is better not to put it as the first or last element, as it may fall apart.

8. **Prepare the barbecue:** The heat shouldn't be too high, as these skewers tend to burn very easily. Before you put them all on to cook, I recommend making a test skewer and observing how quickly it colours – adjust the distance of the grill from the coals accordingly.

9. Cook the skewers for 5 minutes, spacing them a few inches apart. When they start to have a nice amber colour, lightly brush with peach glaze on both sides. Once they are ready, transfer the skewers to a tray.

10. Give them a further gloss with some peach glaze, and finish with a pinch of salt flakes, a few drops of hot sauce, some chives and some sesame seeds. Serve immediately.

SKIRT STEAK, SOUR PLUM, PEARL ONIONS

Serves 6

We have always had a little difficulty serving meat during summer, stuck between the often very hot temperatures, the generous number of customers to serve each service and our preference in this season for vegetables and fish. When we first tried Michele Varvara's skirt steak, however, we were convinced. Nicely browned, flavourful, mineral and juicy: it was perfect for the tasting menu. Its juiciness immediately recalled plums and red wine, with that perfect balance between sweetness and acidity. We serve it slightly chilled, finely sliced like an Asian beef salad, topped with pickled onions, basil, mint and garlic. Our staff used to fight for leftovers and trimmings from this recipe, which is always a very good sign.

Ingredients

1 kg (2 lb 4 oz) beef skirt steak
8 fresh plums, finely sliced
20 g (3/4 oz) lemon juice
25 g (1 oz) Garlic Oil (page 244)
pinch of caster (superfine) sugar
pinch of chilli flakes
150 g (5 oz) Pickled Onions (page 242)
a small bunch of mint and basil leaves
'Nduja Oil (page 244)
salt and freshly ground black pepper

For the plum glaze
1 teaspoon freshly ground black pepper
½ teaspoon fennel seeds
1 star anise
1 clove
110 g (3¾ oz/½ cup) caster sugar
500 lt red wine
600 g (1 lb 5 oz) sour plums, stoned and halved
8 fresh bay leaves

Method

1. **Make the glaze:** Toast the black pepper, fennel seeds, star anise and clove in a small, dry frying pan over a medium heat for 3 minutes, then crush coarsely with a pestle and mortar.

2. In a medium saucepan, make a blond caramel with the sugar. Add the red wine (it will spit a little; that's normal), along with the plums, ground toasted spices and bay leaves. Cook for 1 hour 20 minutes over a low–medium until it has a thick, syrupy consistency.

3. Strain through a sieve, then allow to cool. Keep chilled.

4. **Cook the steak:** Use paper towels to pat dry the skirt steak. Remove all the membranes and part of the fat, then divide the meat into sections of about 200 g (7 oz) each. Season generously with salt and pepper, then leave to rest for 30 minutes at room temperature.

5. Preheat a hibachi grill or barbecue to medium. Cook the steak for 3 to 5 minutes per side (depending on the thickness of the meat), until nicely brown. Bear in mind that skirt steak should be served rare or medium–rare; cooking it for longer would result in it becoming fibrous and dry. If you prefer well-cooked meat, I recommend choosing a different cut.

6. Transfer the meat to a cooling rack and leave to rest for 10 minutes.

7. **Assemble:** Place the sliced plums in a bowl and season with the lemon juice, garlic oil, sugar and chilli flakes, Leave to marinate for a few minutes.

8. Slice the meat, making sure you cut against the grain – this is very important.

9. Arrange the meat on a serving plate and garnish with the Pickled Onions and marinated plums. Just before serving, drizzle with the plum sauce, scatter over the herbs, and finish with a little 'Nduja Oil to taste.

RED MULLET IN FIG LEAF

<u>Serves 6</u>

I have vivid memories of my first summer at Moroseta.
In the afternoons, after lunch service, I would take a walk
in the garden to collect the herbs and produce I would
need for the evening shift. When passing under the fig
trees, which had already absorbed a lot of sunshine and
heat from the morning, I would be stunned by their very
intense essence, absolutely exotic and unknown to my
city girl sense of smell.

Later, I tried to bring back that aroma in different dishes,
hoping to recreate it for my guests. Here, it is combined
with red mullet, which is poetically wrapped in a leaf
and roasted gently over embers, letting the roasted
fragrance that the leaves release once heated come
to the fore. This method of cooking not only ensures a
unique scent, suspended between coconut and coffee,
but also keeps the meat particularly moist and protected
from the open flame. It is simply served with a vinaigrette
made from salted lemon and fig leaf vinegar (for once,
I won't ask you to cook for four hours!).

<u>Ingredients</u>

6 medium-sized red mullets, 350–500g
    (12 oz–1 lb 2 oz) each
12 large fig leaves
extra virgin olive oil, salt

For the vinaigrette
2 small preserved lemons
45 g (1¾ oz/3 tablespoons) Fig Leaf Vinegar (page 74)
20 g (¾ oz/1 tablespoon) honey
200 g (7 oz/scant 1 cup) extra virgin olive oil

Method

1.   Prepare the mullet: Use paper towels to pat dry
   the mullets. Salt them well, inside and out, and
   drizzle with olive oil.

2.   Bring a saucepan of water large enough to hold the
   fig leaves to the boil. Boil the leaves for one minute,
   then drain on paper towels. Leave to cool.

3.   Prepare the vinaigrette: Rinse the salted lemons
   and remove and discard the flesh. Finely chop the
   peel and add it to a bowl or jug with the rest of the
   ingredients. Whisk well to emulsify, then taste and
   set aside.

4.   Assemble and cook: Spread out two fig leaves on
   the work surface, partially overlapping them in the
   centre. Place a mullet in the centre. Fold in the short
   sides of the leaves, then roll up, encasing the mullet
   (a bit like rolling a spring roll). Secure the parcel
   using kitchen twine, preferably starting from the tail.

5.   Prepare the barbecue – you want a medium heat.
   Place the parcels on the grill over indirect medium
   heat, then cover and cook for at least 10–15 minutes.
   Remove from the heat and rest for 4–5 minutes.

6.   I like to serve it still in its leaf packet, having
   removed only the twine. This way, the fish arrives at
   the table still warm and super fragrant. Serve with
   the vinaigrette on the side.

<u>Chef's Notes</u>

Oven option: If you don't have a barbecue, you can cook
this in the oven: 200°C fan (400°F/gas 7) for 15 minutes.

ON GELATO

Of all the variables on our tasting menus, gelato is a solid, undisputed constant. Simple, comforting, but not banal. Italiano, but also universal in its being known and appreciated by all. I tried a few times to temporarily replace it with other recipes, such as a panna cotta, a custard, or a flan, but each time I was met with the question, 'Why is there no gelato today?', both from customers and from myself.

Precisely when gelato became such a distinctive symbol of what we do, I cannot say. It was a natural, unintentional evolution. As for the why, there are many reasons.

Over the years, we have done various pop-up dinners and events abroad, and I have always insisted on making gelato, even in the most extreme of situations. As it had become a symbol of our cuisine, I knew that everyone expected it in some way. This led me to gelato adventures of no small magnitude, such as churning in an open-air courtyard in the middle of winter because the kitchen was too hot to set the gelato.

In Copenhagen, I sent a taxi at the last minute to pick up a gelato machine kindly loaned by a chef friend, because our one had broken. In Milan I asked (or, more honestly, begged) to be allowed to keep the gelato in the freezer of a restaurant a few blocks away from where I was doing the event. Luckily, the owners of the restaurant were from Puglia, and welcomed my crazy request.

Finally, at the airport in London, I had to explain that those unlabelled sachets of yellow powder were wild fennel pollen, collected and dried during the summer, which I needed to flavour a gelato I was dying to make.

Well, it was always worth it.

PEA POD

In spring, when we use large quantities of peas, we make a
fiordilatte base by infusing all the leftover pea pods in hot
milk, which is then blended and sieved to get all the flavour.

CHERRY SORBET

Marion, a talented French chef I worked with in my early years
of cooking, taught me how to make the best cherry sorbet ever.
The secret lies in blending the fruit with the whole stone, which will
give the base an incredible depth with notes of bitter almond
on the finish.

SICILIAN MANGO, LIME, SPICY HONEY AND SALT

In late summer, organic Sicilian mangoes arrive, like a last gift
from nature before it moves on to autumn ingredients. Their silky
and super-aromatic pulp becomes a delicious gelato. We add lime
juice, Spicy Honey (page 237) and a hint of salt, and serve it with an
dark chocolate ganache, extra virgin olive oil and more salt.

FIG LEAF

Fig leaves are great in gelato even if not roasted, when they
have a more herbaceous aroma. They're perfect in a fior di latte
base, a yoghurt base for an acid kick, or in a custard base for
a super-decadent result.

FRESH POLLEN

Pollen is an ingredient that fascinates me so much; its complex and
nuanced aroma is truly unique. When we find it fresh, we use it in a
yoghurt-based gelato which balances the pollen's mellow sweetness.

FIG LEAF GELATO,
APRICOT SORBET

Makes 1 kg/2 lb 4 oz each

Gelato is never missing in our kitchen, but it undoubtedly knows its peak moment in summer. I have already spoken about the magic of the fig leaf, but when used in the base of a gelato, it can really give great surprises. To complement the toasted roundness of the fig leaf, we combine it with a very fresh apricot sorbet, made even fresher by cardamom. They are also excellent individually, but together they create a truly unique mix, an ode to summer in the form of gelato.

Ingredients

For the fig leaf gelato:
110 g (3¾ oz) fresh fig leaves
680 g (1 lb 8 oz/2¾ cups) milk
150 g (5 oz/⅔ cup) fresh cream
135 g (4 ¾ oz/scant ⅔ cup) caster sugar
40 g (1½ oz) honey
4 g (¼ oz) carob seed powder
2 g (⅛ oz) salt

For the apricot sorbet:
5 cardamom pods
170 g (6 oz/¾ cup) caster (superfine) sugar
300 g (10½ oz/1¼ cups) water
3 g (⅛ oz) carob seed powder
700 g (1 lb 9 oz) apricots
60 g (2 oz/¼ cup) fresh lemon juice
35 g (1¼ oz) honey

Method

1. Make the fig leaf gelato: Preheat the oven to 160°C fan (320°F/gas 4).

2. Spread out the fig leaves a baking tray and toast them in the oven for 15–20 minutes, turning after 10 minutes, so that they all dry evenly. They should start to brown slightly, dry out and smell toasty. Leave to cool at room temperature, well spaced out.

3. In a saucepan over a low heat, heat the milk to about 50°C (122°F). Take off the heat, then add the fig leaves, crumbling them coarsely with your hands. Stir well, then cover the pan and infuse for 2 hours.

4. Strain through a sieve and press well. Weigh the milk and check that you still have 680 g (1 lb 8 oz/ 2¾ cups); it may have decreased considerably, as fig leaves tend to absorb a lot of liquid.

5. Top up any missing milk, then pour it all into a medium saucepan and add the cream. Heat over a low–medium until it reaches 40°C (104°F), then add the other ingredients. Continue cooking until the mixture reaches 85°C (185°F), stirring often.

6. Take the pan off the heat, and blend with an hand blender for a few seconds, then transfer into a container with a lid. Cool quickly with a blast chiller or in an ice bath. Once cold, leave in the refrigerator for 12 hours.

7. The following day, you will notice that the mixture is thicker and a little elastic. Blend for a few seconds and then add to your gelato machine and churn according to the manufacturer's instructions.

8. Make the apricot sorbet: In a dry frying pan over a medium heat, toast the cardamom pods for a couple of minutes until fragrant. Transfer them to a pestle and mortar and crush with 2 tablespoons of the sugar.

9. Heat the water in a saucepan over a low heat. Gradually add the rest of the sugar and cardamom mix and the carob seed powder. Continue cooking until the mixture reaches 85°C (185°F), stirring often. Strain to remove the cardamom pieces, then pour the resulting syrup into a container and cool down quickly in an ice bath as above.

10. Meanwhile, wash the apricots, then remove the kernels and any dark spots. In a blender, blend the fruit and lemon juice until you get a smooth purée.

11. Once the syrup is cold, add it to the purée and mix for a few seconds with a hand blender. Transfer to the refrigerator and chill for 12 hours.

12. The following day, blend again for a few seconds, then add to your gelato machine and churn according to the manufacturer's instructions.

13. Serve a generous scoop of each in a chilled glass.

Serves 8

For some time at the beginning of my career in kitchens, I dedicated myself to desserts, specifically complex restaurant desserts: a thousand different preparations, including creams, sauces, crumbles, sponges, granitas, sorbets and jellies. At the time, I loved it. I felt great satisfaction at mastering that variety of complicated elements. My palate, however, was looking for something different; my perfect dessert was disarmingly simple, yet refined in its balance of flavours.

The peach galette represents this concept pretty well. My requirements: fine, buttery, slightly salty crust, rolled out very thin. A generous layer of perfectly ripe peaches, sliced with precision Cooked until perfectly caramelised on the edges, with a concentration of fruit juices for a perfect balance of sweetness and acidity. It should be eaten immediately, within a couple of hours at the most, otherwise the careful balance will gradually be lost as moisture compromises this perfect architecture. Have I convinced you?

Ingredients

For the crust
5 g (¼ oz/2 teaspoons) fennel seeds,
    plus extra for sprinkling
180 g (6½ oz/1½ cups) flour, plus extra for dusting
35 g (1¼ oz/generous ¼ cup) wholemeal spelt flour
15 g (½ oz/generous 1 tablespoon) cane sugar,
    plus extra for sprinkling
pinch of salt
25 g (1 oz/¼ cup) almond flour
30 g (1 oz/2 tablespoons) milk
30 g (1 oz/2 tablespoons) yoghurt
5 g (¼ oz/1 teaspoon) apple cider vinegar
2–3 tablespoons ice-cold water
110 g (3¾ oz) butter, cut into small cubes
1 egg, beaten, for egg wash

For the filling
4 medium-sized peaches, not too ripe
juice of 1 lemon
30 g (1 oz/generous 2 tablespoons) cane sugar
100 g (3½ oz) peach compote

To finish
60 g (2 oz) Brown Butter (page 233)

Method

1. Prepare the crust: In a small, dry frying pan, toast the fennel seeds over a medium heat for a couple of minutes until fragrant (don't let them brown too much!). Allow to cool, then coarsely grind with a pestle and mortar.

2. Sift the flours into a medium bowl, and mix in the sugar, salt, ground almonds and ground fennel seeds. Add the butter and, working with your fingers, rub it in until you get a sandy texture.

3. In another bowl, whisk together the milk, yoghurt, vinegar and a couple of tablespoons of ice-cold water. Drizzle this mixture over the flour mixture and mix with a spatula until the dough starts coming together. if it's too dry, you can add some more water (use a tablespoon – if you add too much, there is no way back!).

4. Transfer to a floured surface and knead gently until smooth. Shape into a disc about 2 cm (¾ in) thick, wrap in cling film (plastic wrap) and leave to chill in the refrigerator for 2 hours.

5. Prepare the peaches: Preheat the oven to 170°C fan (340°F/gas 5) and line a baking tray with a silicone mat.

6. Wash and peel the peaches. Halve each one, remove the stone and cut the flesh in thin, regular slices, trying to keep their original shape. Arrange the slices spaced out on the prepared baking tray. Brush each peach with the lemon juice and sprinkle with the sugar. Bake for 15 minutes, then leave to cool.

7. Assemble and bake: Preheat the oven to 175°C (350°F/gas 6) and line a large, rimmed baking sheet with baking parchment. Remove the dough from the refrigerator and leave to rest for 5 minutes at room temperature. Transfer to a lightly floured surface and roll out into a (kinda) regular round, about 28–30 cm (11–12 in) in diameter. To keep it from sticking, rotate often and dust with more flour as needed.

→   Continued on Following Page

8.   Transfer the dough to the prepared baking sheet. (If the dough is too soft, let it chill for 10 minutes before assembling).

9.   Leave a 5 cm (2 in) border around the edges, and prick the rest of the surface of the dough with a fork. Spread the peach compote over the dough in a thin, even layer, and arrange the peach slices on top, overlapping slightly. Gently fold the border over the peaches, tucking in as needed. Finish with a light brushing of beaten egg on the borders, then sprinkle everything with some more cane sugar and fennel seeds. Bake, rotating once, for 35 minutes.

10.   Meanwhile, melt the butter in a small saucepan over a medium heat. Let it foam and then brown, stirring often. Cook for 5–7 minutes until it smells nutty (be careful not to burn it). Remove from the heat, strain through a sieve and leave to cool at room temperature.

11.   After 35 minutes, the galette's crust should be golden brown and the peaches soft and juicy. Brush the whole galette with the Brown Butter and leave to cool for at least 45 minutes before slicing. Serve with whipped cream or gelato.

Chef's Notes

Compote: The use of compote or jam is not mandatory, but I find that it creates a good binder between fruit and crust. Since the layer is rather thin, the taste doesn't affect it much – you can just use whatever type you have available.

Storage: This will keep for up to 3 days, covered and stored at room temperature, but it will start softening after the first day.

APRICOT COMPOTE

Makes 3 x 250 g (8¾ oz) jars

Summer fruit is particularly ideal for making compote, cooked quickly and gently to keep the flavours as intact and clean as possible. We flavour this apricot compote with its own kernels, which have an extraordinary natural aroma similar to amaretto.

Compotes are extraordinary for breakfast. Our favourite combination from last summer was suggested by our colleague Antony, who had us try some lightly toasted focaccia topped with fresh ricotta and apricot compote—*uncroyable*, as Antony would say with a distinct Quebecois accent.

Ingredients

For the compote
1 kg (2 lb 4 oz) apricots
200 g (7 oz/scant 1 cup) caster (superfine) sugar
juice of 1 lemon

Method

1. Wash the apricots, then remove the stones (keep them aside) and any dark spots. Cut the flesh into regular pieces, then add to a large bowl with the sugar and lemon juice. Mix well, then cover and leave to rest for 20 minutes.

2. Meanwhile, crush the apricot stones using a pestle and mortar and obtain 5 small kernels, trying not to break them up too much.

3. Add the kernels to the fruit and sugar mixture, then transfer it all into a saucepan over a low–medium heat. Cook for about 25 minutes, stirring often, then bring to boil. Reduce the heat and simmer gently for a further 5 minutes.

4. Pour the compote into sterilised jars and close with new lids. Sterilise again and store in the pantry. The shelf life of a compote, which contains far less sugar than a classic jam, is about 3 months.

5. If you intend to use it up quickly, you don't need to sterilise the jars; you can just store the compote directly in the refrigerator once ready.

MOROSETA

MANU'S TOMATO SAUCE

Makes 4 × 750 ml (25 fl oz/3 cup) bottles

If we were to make any Italian grandmother in southern Italy read this recipe, it would create no small amount of controversy: 'What do you mean, "Cook for four hours"?'; 'Lemon, did you say *lemon*?'; 'What do you do with all that *sofrito*?'; 'Sugar, are you kidding me?'. Those would be some of the questions that would be asked, without hesitation.

There are many golden laws when it comes to the sacred process of making tomato sauce; Manu decides to observe basically none of them, choosing his own personal approach. For my part, I can tell you that this is no ordinary tomato sauce. There is complexity, technique, love and much more. In the kitchen, we guard it jealously. A few bottles are produced each year, to be kept aside and used parsimoniously until the following summer.

Ingredients

For the sauce
120 g (4¼ oz) olive oil
3 onions (about 500 g/1 lb 2 oz in total), finely sliced
4 kg (8 lb 12 oz) mixed tomatoes, roughly chopped
    unless small
bunch of basil
45 g (1¾ oz/scant ¼ cup) caster (superfine) sugar
zest of 3 lemons
salt

Method

1. Heat the oil in a large saucepan over a low–medium heat. Add the onions and cook for 15 minutes until they are translucent and soft, but not browned.

2. Add the tomatoes, season with salt, and increase the heat to medium. Cook for 5 minutes, so that the tomatoes start to collapse and release their water. Reduce the heat to very low, then add the basil and sugar. Simmer gently for 4 hours, stirring occasionally.

3. After this, the mixture should have reduced by more than half. Add the lemon zest at the end of the cooking time, then leave to cool.

4. Once cool, transfer to a blender and blend at high speed until you get a smooth purée. Taste and adjust the seasoning. If it is too thick, you can add a little water while blending.

5. Pour the sauce into sterilised bottles or jars and close with new lids.

03 AUTUMN

Autumn in Puglia is quite different from the common perception of the season. We are usually graced with beautiful days and mild temperatures until mid-November, with a warm and embracing colour palette. But once the weather turns, the first autumn ingredients to appear on market stalls are bitter greens, such as chicory and puntarelle, cardoncelli mushrooms, pumpkins and root vegetables such as beetroot and heirloom carrots. It is also the time of the olive harvest: for three weeks, our team of gardeners are dedicated to picking olives from our centuries-old trees.

Creatively, after months of ice-cold soups, broths and copious salads we can start taking back control with cooking, creating contrasts, textures and exploring slow cooking. Pumpkin, Jerusalem artichoke, celeriac and beetroot are perfect bases for strong contrasts, higher acidity and deep roasting.

PICKLED SHIITAKE AND
CARDONCELLI MUSHROOMS

Makes 1.2 kg (2 lb 6 oz)

This preparation is a classic of the autumn season at Moroseta kitchen. We use shiitake and cardoncelli mushrooms, fresh and organically produced in Puglia: real gems. Manu has fine-tuned this recipe by layering different umami elements, for a complex, delicious and mouthwatering result. We start by roasting the mushrooms in the oven to release all the umami potential, before marinating them in an Asian-inspired sauce with miso, shoyu and sesame oil.

Consider this a secret weapon to always have at hand, perfect for when you need to elevate delicate ingredients or fix unconvincing preparations, just like a good piece of Parmigiano.

Ingredients

1.2 kg (2 lb 10 oz) medium/small shiitake
    and cardoncelli mushrooms
40 g (1½ oz/3 tablespoons) olive oil
6 g (¼ oz) salt

For the marinade
20 g (¾ oz) barley miso
40 g (1½ oz) shoyu soy sauce
40 g (1½ oz/2¾ tablespoons) rice vinegar
15 g (½ oz/¾ tablespoon) honey
15 g (½ oz/1¼ tablespoons) toasted sesame oil
50 g (2 oz/3¾ tablespoons) extra virgin olive oil
bunch of thyme
4 fresh bay leaves
3 garlic cloves, peeled

Method

1. Roast the mushrooms: Preheat the oven to 210°C (410°F/gas 8).

2. Clean the mushrooms carefully, using damp paper towels or a brush to remove dirt and soil. It is best to never wash them under running water. Cut the larger mushrooms in half, while leaving the smaller ones whole.

3. In a bowl, combine the mushrooms with the oil and salt, massaging well, then arrange them on several baking trays, ensuring they are well spread out. It is important that they are not too close together, because steam would be created, compromising even browning.

4. Roast in the oven for 15–20 minutes until the mushrooms are cooked through and golden brown. If they could do with a little more colour, pop them under the grill (broiler) for a few minutes until they are golden brown and fragrant. Set aside.

5. Marinate: In a jug or bowl, dissolve the miso and honey in the vinegar and shoyu, then emulsify with the oils.

6. Put the mushrooms into a container with the herbs and peeled garlic cloves, then pour over the marinade. Mix well and cover. Leave to marinate in the refrigerator for 24 hours before using.

Chef's Notes

How to use them: These mushrooms are quite powerful, a real concentration of flavour. I recommend using them as an umami carrier in other recipes. They can be combined with whipped ricotta and hazelnuts for a super-yummy bruschetta; they can enrich a classic risotto alla parmigiana; they can garnish a fried egg with sautéed spinach. You could even finely chop them, then mix with cooked potatoes and Parmesan to make a filling for ravioli or cabbage rolls.

Mushroom varieties: This is a recipe that lends itself to all kinds of mushrooms, but I would not use rare expensive mushrooms; the seasoning would just cover their flavour. On the contrary, it lends itself particularly well to rather neutral mushrooms.

BEET, ALMOND, BOTTARGA

Serves 6

In early October, we find wonderful, coloured beets, very tender and silky, perfect to serve as a starter. Their sweet nature lends itself to contrasting savoury flavours – in this case, our beloved bottarga, refreshed by the acidity of our homemade carpione vinegar. In order not to spoil the aesthetic appearance of this root, and to create a surprise effect, this dish is composed in reverse, starting with the sauces and ending with a mosaic of shiny beet slices. Consistencies and flavours come together in an interesting and unexpected balance, vaguely recalling the effect of a *vitello tonnato*. Hard to imagine, but I can assure you that this is exactly how it feels.

Ingredients

8 medium-sized beetroots in mixed colours
60 g (2 oz) almonds
salt

For the carpione vinaigrette
50 g (2 oz) Carpione Vinegar (page 244)
12 g (½ oz/½ tablespoon) mild honey
60 g (2 oz/¼ cup) olive oil
60 g (2 oz/¼ cup) grapeseed oil
5 g (¼ oz) salt

For the almond and bottarga emulsion
180 g (6½ oz) Almond Emulsion (page 232)
5 g (¼ oz) colatura d'alici
20 g (¾ oz) grated bottarga (see Chef's Notes)

To finish
zest of 1 lemon
chopped chives
30 g (1 oz) grated bottarga

Method

1. **Steam the beetroots:** Steam the beetroots over a medium-low heat. Check the consistency after 20 minutes; they should be cooked but still firm. The cooking time can vary a lot depending on the size and type of beetroot.

2. Once ready, rub them with your hands or paper towel to remove the skin; it should come off easily. Let cool and refrigerate for 1 hour.

3. **Prepare the elements:** In a bowl or jug, mix the almond emulsion with the grated bottarga and colatura. Place in a squeezing bottle and set aside.

4. Preheat the oven to 160°C fan (320°F/gas 4). Toast the almonds for 10–12 minutes, then finely chop and set aside.

5. Using a mandoline, slice the cooled beetroots into 3 mm (⅛ in) slices . Start with the lighter-coloured ones, so they don't get stained by the darker ones. Arrange the beetroot slices on trays, separating the layers with baking parchment. Keep in the refrigerator until ready to use.

6. About 10 minutes before serving, season the beetroots with the vinaigrette and a pinch of salt. Brush the dressing over them so that it penetrates evenly. Taste them before serving to make sure they have absorbed the dressing.

7. **Assemble:** Draw a spiral of almond emulsion on each plate, then scatter some chopped almonds, chives and freshly grated lemon zest on top. Add a few drops of vinaigrette. It is important that everything is fairly flat. Using an offset spatula, arrange the beetroot slices on top, alternating different colours and sizes. Serve immediately.

Chef's Notes

Bottarga: If you have difficulty finding bottarga, you can replace it with anchovy paste, or use white miso for a vegan substitute.

CHICKEN LIVER PÂTÉ

Makes 800 g (1 lb 12 oz)

Our bread service, which in summer shows juicy vegetables, legume dip and local fresh cheeses, becomes more classic in autumn, a tribute to *antipasto all'italiana*. The main protagonist is the pâté, served as a whipped cloud to be spread generously on brioche bread alongside homemade pickles.

Ingredients

500 g (1 lb 2 oz) chicken livers
15 g (½ oz) juniper berries
120 g (4¼ oz/generous ⅓ cup) coarse salt
410 g (14½ oz) butter
250 g (9 oz) onions, very thinly sliced
180 g (6½ oz/¾ cup) sweet wine

Method

1. Prepare the livers: Clean the livers by removing all the membranes and connective tissues.

2. In a dry frying pan over a low-medium heat, toast the juniper berries for a couple of minutes until shiny and fragrant. Tip into a small blender and blend with the salt for 20 seconds until you get coarse paste. Place the livers in a container, cover evenly with the aromatic salt and leave to rest for 40 minutes.

3. Make the pâté: Meanwhile, melt 60 g (2 oz) of the butter in a medium-sized saucepan over a medium-low heat. Add the onions and wilt gently for 15 minutes. Deglaze with the sweet wine and cook for a few minutes more to allow the alcohol to evaporate.

4. Rinse the salt off the livers and pat dry with a paper towel. Add the livers to the pan with the cooked onions, and cook over a medium heat for 20 minutes.

5. Transfer into a blender and add the remaining 350g (12 oz) butter. Blend well until fully emulsified. Pass through a muslin (cheesecloth) to achieve a super-smooth consistency, then transfer to a container. Cover the surface with cling film (plastic wrap) to prevent oxidation. Refrigerate for at least 3 hours before serving. This can be served as it is, or whipped in the stand mixer for a few minutes, if you prefer a fluffy texture.

AMBERJACK,
CITRUS, KIMCHI

Serves 6

Regardless of the season, crudo is never missing from
our tasting menu. We consider it the ideal way to start
a special meal, an essential element. A small quantity
of really good fish, well seasoned and served at the
right temperature, puts you in the right mood to enjoy
the rest of the experience. It feels special, refined, but
also quintessentially Puglia. Here, we combine the silky
roundness of the amberjack of the Adriatic sea with the
first citrus fruits from our garden, with a side kick of
kimchi to spice things up a bit.

Ingredients

300 g (10½ oz) amberjack fillet
8 kumquats
pinch of sugar
Bay Leaf Oil (page 243), for drizzling
a few chervil leaves, to serve
salt

For the sauce
100 g (3½ oz/scant ½ cup) kimchi juice
70 g (2¼ oz) Candied Citrus Paste (page 234)
30 g (1 oz/2 tablespoons) clementine juice
3 g (⅛ oz/½ teaspoon) salt

Method

1. Prepare the amberjack: Remove the skin and
   any bones from the fish fillet. Salt generously on
   both sides (see Chef's Notes). Leave to rest for
   20 minutes, then dry well with paper towels. Leave
   to rest, uncovered, in the refrigerator for 3 hours
   (up to overnight).

2. Make the sauce and macerate the kumquats:
   In a bowl, mix together all the ingredients for the
   sauce. Taste – if it is too intense, it can be diluted
   by gradually adding water.

3. Slice the kumquats, removing any seeds. Place in a
   shallow bowl and season with a pinch each of salt
   and sugar. Leave to macerate for 15 minutes.

4. Assemble: Slice the fish into even slices, and divide
   between six chilled plates, alternating fish slices
   with marinated kumquat slices.

5. Pour a spoonful of the cold sauce into the base of
   each plate, then finish with a little bay leaf oil and a
   few leaves of fresh chervil.

Chef's Notes

Salting Fish: Ever since we started applying this
technique of salting fish in advance, we haven't gone
back. First of all, it improves the texture; the fish will lose
some of its moisture, firming up considerably. Moreover,
this way, the salt penetrates evenly, meaning the fish
is not salted only on the surface, but throughout. The
thicker the fillet, the longer this salting process will take.
Start step by step and taste each time. If you like, the
salt can be flavoured with herbs or spices.

BEEF TARTARE, BLACK GARLIC, DAIKON, NASTURTIUM

Serves 6

For a while, as much as I love a good tartare, we couldn't serve it. Finding really good meat, raised in the best way, treated with respect and knowledge, had become an impossible task. Then, when we started working with Michele Varvara, everything changed. He is a rare person, very passionate, always up to date, and with a unique respect for the animal. It is not we who order the meat, it is he who proposes what he can provide, according to the season and availability.

Ingredients

270 g (9½ oz) beef tenderloin, preferably
    dry-aged for one month
60 g (2 oz) Winter Giardinera (page 187)
90 g (3¼ oz) Black Garlic Emulsion (page 235)
42 g (1½ oz) buckwheat groats
30 g (1 oz) Soy and Wine Glaze (page 236)
30 g (1 oz) Bay Leaf Oil (page 243)
50 g (2 oz) Garlic Oil (page 244)
nasturtium leaves, to serve
salt, freshly ground black pepper

Method

1. Prepare the tartare: Trim the beef of fat and connective tissues, trying waste as little as possible. Cut into thin slices, then cut each slice into strips and then into small cubes. It is important to use a good sharp knife, so as not to stress the meat too much.

2. Seal the tartare in foil and refrigerate until ready to use; it is important that it does not exposed to the light, otherwise it will darken.

3. Prepare the other elements: Preheat the oven to 170°C fan (340°F/gas 5). Scatter the buckwheat on to a baking tray and toast in the oven for 10–15 minutes, stirring every 5 minutes, until it browns and gives off a distinctly toasted aroma.

4. Cut the daikon into similar-sized pieces and set aside in its pickling liquid.

5. Place the black garlic emulsion into a small piping bag.

6. Assemble: Put the meat tartare into a bowl and season gently with the garlic oil and some salt and pepper. Taste and adjust as needed; keep the seasoning light, as we are going to add more elements on top.

7. Divide between six plates, giving it a regular but not too precise shape. Add a few small dots of black garlic emulsion to each plate, along with a few drops of glaze and bay leaf oil. Finish by adding few cubes of daikon, the scatter over the buckwheat and nasturtium leaves and serve.

Chef's Notes

Keep it simple: I am aware that there are a good number of ingredients and oils involved in this recipe. The fundamental element, in my opinion, is the black garlic emulsion; the others can be considered benefits that fit in very well, but are not essential.

Serves 6

This is a recipe with special personal significance. Ten years ago, I was an insecure and average intern in the kitchen of Erba Brusca in Milan. I hoped to be able to stand in a corner and observe, maybe peel some potatoes, without having my technical deficiency noticed too much. Instead, Chef Alice immediately put me to work, entrusting me with the starters section. One of the dishes was this soup, which I learned to make after a few unsuccessful attempts. Every time I smell the sweet scent of celeriac simmering with apples and bay leaf, my mind goes back to those scary and exciting early days of my career in the kitchen in a very foggy Milano, when everything looked extremely difficult and new – even a soup. This version remains faithful to Alice's combination of flavours, while varying in technique and final result.

Ingredients

1.5 kg (3 lb 5 oz) celeriac, peeled and roots removed
30 g (1 oz) butter
3 small onions, finely sliced
2 bay leaves
2 apples, peeled, cored and cut into wedges
50 g (2 oz) Brown Butter (see page 233)
12 g (½ oz/scant 1 tablespoon) apple cider vinegar
salt, freshly ground black pepper

For the celeriac confit
500 ml (17 fl oz/2 cups) grape seed oil
500 g (1 lb 2 oz) celeriac, peeled and roots removed, diced into 5 mm (¼ in) cubes (300 g/10½ oz prepared weight)
2 garlic cloves, peeled
lemon juice, to taste

To serve
marjoram leaves
Bay Leaf Oil (page 243)

Method

1. Make the soup: Preheat the oven to 210°C fan (410°F/gas 8).

2. Chop the celeriac into large pieces and arrange on a baking tray without seasoning. Roast in the oven for 15 minutes until golden brown (see Chef's Notes).

3. Melt the butter in a medium-sized saucepan over a low heat. Add the onions and bay leaves and wilt gently for 10 minutes, then add the apples and the toasted celeriac. Season with salt and cook for a further 5 minutes, turning up the heat a little.

4. Barely cover with hot water, then bring to the boil and cook for 35 minutes. Take care that some liquid remains in the pan, adding more water as needed.

5. Transfer to a blender and add the brown butter and vinegar. Blend at maximum speed for 2 minutes until emulsified. Taste and adjust the seasoning and consistency as needed.

6. Make the confit: In a medium-sized saucepan over a low heat, heat the grapeseed oil to 60°C (140°F). Add the celeriac cubes and peeled garlic cloves. Cook at a constant temperature for 10–15 minutes. The celeriac cubes should become translucent, but still retain a nice texture. Remove from the oil with a slotted spoon and set aside.

7. Assemble: Season the celeriac confit with a pinch of salt and pepper and a few drops of lemon juice. Divide between six warm bowls and cover with a ladleful of hot soup. The cubes should be hidden; they will be a surprise as guests taste the dish. Finish with marjoram leaves and Bay Leaf Oil.

Chef's Notes

Technique: Roasting vegetables before making a soup or purée allows you to concentrate the flavours, especially if they are relatively sweet vegetables. If you want to keep the flavours more delicate, you can skip this step.

KIMCHI TORTELLINI,
CELERIAC BROTH, KOMBU

Serves 6

As soon as September ends, I start impatiently awaiting the day when I will finally eat a bowl of *tortellini in brodo*. Steaming hot, it is comfort food by definition and my equivalent for Proust's madeleine.

This version is vegetarian, with the umami component guaranteed thanks to the use of kimchi, Parmesan and seaweed. These tortellini were last winter's must-eat. We made them for weeks, and I enjoyed watching customers' expressions from the kitchen; how they exchanging surprised looks and nodding their heads between bites.

Ingredients

For the broth
1 kg (2 lb 4 oz) celeriac
15 g (½ oz) roasted seaweed (mix of kombu and dulse)
1.5 litres (51 fl oz/6 cups) boiling water
lemon juice, to taste
salt

For the pasta
200 g (7 oz/scant 1⅔ cups) '00' flour
50 g (2 oz/scant ½ cup) semolina flour
3 g (⅛ oz/½ teaspoon) salt
1 small egg (about 40 g/1½ oz)
7 egg yolks (about 140 g/4¾ oz)
10 g (½ oz/2 teaspoons) olive oil

For the kimchi paste
6 g (¼ oz/1½ teaspoons) toasted sesame oil
30 g (1 oz/2¼ tablespoons) olive oil
50 g (2 oz) onion, sliced
1 garlic clove
10 g (½ oz) fresh ginger, peeled and finely sliced
50 g (2 oz) finely chopped carrot
100 g (3½ oz) savoy cabbage, finely chopped
150 g (5 oz) fresh kimchi

For the filling
230 g (8¼ oz) stale bread without crusts
60 g (2 oz) grated Parmesan
1 egg, beaten

To finish
Garlic Brown Butter (page 233)

Method

1. Make the broth: Preheat the oven to 200°C fan (400°F/gas 6).

2.   Roughly chop the celeriac into big chunks, then tip into a blender. Blend until you get a wet, sandy texture (be careful; if you blend it too much, it will turn almost to liquid).

3. Spread out this mixture on a large baking tray and roast for about 30 minutes, stirring every 10 minutes to make sure the edges do not burn. Once evenly roasted, it should be fragrant with a soil-like texture, and will have lost most of its moisture.

4. Combine the roasted celeriac and seaweed in a large bowl and pour in the boiling water. Stir well and leave to infuse, covered, for 6 hours.

5. Make the pasta dough: Mix the flour and semolina in the bowl of a stand mixer and add the salt. In a jug, beat together the egg, egg yolks and oil. Slowly add the liquids to the dry ingredients and knead on a medium speed for 7–10 minutes. The dough should be elastic and perfectly combined.

6. Cover with cling film (plastic wrap) and leave to rest for at least 4 hours in the refrigerator.

7. Make the kimchi paste: Meanwhile, heat the olive and sesame oils in a medium-sized saucepan over a medium-low heat. Add the onion and garlic and sauté for 8 minutes until golden brown. Add the ginger, carrot and cabbage, and sauté for a few minutes. Add the kimchi and cook for 15 minutes, taking care to dry out all the moisture. Set aside.

8. Make the filling: Quickly blend the stale bread into rough breadcrumbs. Add the Parmesan and kimchi paste, and combine until you get a firm mixture. If it looks too dry (this depends on the dryness of the bread used), you can add some beaten egg. Leave to rest for at least 2 hours to allow the dough to rehydrate.

→   Continued on Following Page

9. Make the tortellini: Roll out the dough with the help of a pasta machine, making it as thin as possible; you need to be able to almost see through it.

10. Once rolled out, cut into 4 cm (1½ in) squares and distribute the filling in small knobs in the centre of each square. Moisten the edges of one of the squares with a little water and fold diagonally into a triangle shape, making sure to tightly encase the filling without leaving air bubbles. Now join the two bottom corners together into the classic tortellini shape. Proceed with the other squares and filling until you run out of ingredients.

11. Place the filled tortellini on a tray, well spaced out and covered with a clean tea towel.

12. Assemble: Strain the broth through a sieve, pressing well to extract as much flavour as possible. Taste the strained broth; if you feel it is not intense enough, you can reduce it by simmering gently for half an hour. Add salt if needed, and adjust the acidity with a few drops of lemon. If not reducing, reheat the broth over a low heat.

13. Cook the tortellini in a pan of boiling salted water for about 3 minutes, then drain and divide between six warm bowls. Cover with the hot broth and finish with some garlic brown butter.

MOROSETA

CIME DI RAPA RISOTTO

Serves 6

Around mid-November, cime di rapa (turnip greens), the most iconic and beloved vegetable of this region, begin their season. Market stalls fill up with these verdant bundles and vendors compete to show who has the prettiest ones, showing off their beautiful florets. It is a very representative vegetable of Puglia, full of character and strength, yet humble in its simple nature.

Ingredients

1.2 kg (2 lb 6 oz) cime di rapa (turnip greens)
250 g (¾ oz) Carnaroli rice
60 g (2¼ oz) white wine
80 g (2¾ oz) Beurre Blanc (page 232)
40 g (1½ oz) pecorino, grated
30 g (1 oz) Parmesan, grated

For the cime di rapa cream
1 onion
1 small pear
50 g (1¾ oz) olive oil
2 bay leaves
100 g (3½ oz) dry white wine
blanched cime di rapa leaves

To finish
Garlic Oil (page 244)
1 lemon
Bread crust powder (see notes)
cime di rapa flowers
30 g Black Olive Caramel (page 219)

Method

1. Start by cleaning the cime di rapa: Separate the florets from the leaves, discarding the most fibrous and tough part of the stems. Bring a medium-sized pan of salted water to the boil, then start by cooking the leaves for five minutes, until tender. Cool in an ice bath, squeeze out the excess water and keep aside, leaving the cooking water on the heat for the florets. Next, blanch the florets for about 3 minutes. Cool in a ice bath and place on a tray on kitchen paper to absorb excess moisture. Reserve the cooking water, as this will be used to cook the rice.

2. For the cime di rapa cream: Finely slice the onion, peel the pear, remove the core and cut into chunks.

3. In a medium-small saucepan, heat the oil, add the onion, bay leaves and a good pinch of salt, cook for 10 minutes until translucent and lightly golden. Add the pear, cook for 3 minutes and deglaze with wine. Reduce the heat to low and cook for 12 minutes until the mixture is cooked through and even. Keep warm.

4. In a blender, blend the onion and pear mix, discarding the bay leaf, with the blanched cime di rapa leaves and a few drops of lemon juice. Blend at maximum speed until smooth and the consistency of single cream. A little cooking water can be added, if the cream is too thick. Cover and set aside.

5. For the risotto: Prepare the florets that will go on top of the risotto to serve. Drizzle the florets with oil and grill for about 2 minutes on both sides. Place on a small tray and season with a few drops of garlic oil, lemon juice, some zest and flaky salt, taste and adjust seasoning. Keep warm until ready to use.

6. Heat the water used to cook the cime di rapa, check that it is well seasoned and keep at a gentle simmer. In a medium-sized saucepan, toast the rice with a little oil for about 4 minutes over medium heat. Deglaze with wine, allow the alcohol to evaporate for a minute and start cooking by adding a ladle of cooking water, it should just barely cover the rice. Stir frequently, and when it starts to dry up, add another ladleful. After the first 7 minutes, start adding the cime di rapa cream, adding it in three stages, always alternating with some broth. The cooking time varies depending on the quality of the rice, it can range from 13–18 minutes. At the end of the cooking time, off the heat add Beurre Blanc, Parmesan and pecorino, then leave covered for 2 minutes. Stir and add a little broth if needed.

7. Divide among 6 plates, garnish each plate with a few grilled florets, about a teaspoon per person of Black Olive Caramel and lightly dust with Bread Crust Powder and cime di rapa flowers, if you have them, then serve immediately.

ON PUMPKIN

The arrival of pumpkin represents the beginning of my favourite season. Widely grown and used in northern Italy, I discovered to my delight that pumpkins also grow very well in Puglia, even though they are not part of the local agricultural tradition. Our trusted supplier Antonio starts with the first Hokkaido ones as early as late August; grown in a semi-arid culture, they are dense and richly flavourful.

My favourite is the Marina di Chioggia, also called 'Iron Cup'. It is super dense and very sweet, with a taste reminiscent of fresh chestnuts. It is traditionally used to make ravioli, combining the pumpkin pulp with plenty of Parmesan cheese, mostarda and amaretti biscuits for a totally unique combination of flavours.

One of the most interesting aspects of pumpkins is their versatility; they can be easily employed in both sweet and savoury dishes. You can decide to use the natural sweetness as a fantastic base for acidity, smokiness and spiciness, or play with a layering of sweetness and roundness, working with warm, enveloping spices, butter and dried fruits.

Perhaps the trickiest part is the cutting; their large size and hard flesh can make things difficult. At Moroseta, we use two techniques. The first involves cutting one side so that there is a flat, stable, supporting surface, and then portioning it off. The other involves placing the squash in the oven for 10 minutes so that it softens on the outside, meaning the knife can cut through it more easily.

Some pumpkins, such as butternut squash, do not require peeling, especially when they are small and young. Their skin is thin and edible, even when raw.

PUMPKIN AND MATURE CHEESE

Pumpkin, by its very nature sweet and accommodating, is greatly
enhanced by the savouriness of mature cheese, from classic Parmesan
to the most robust of blue cheeses. This combination of flavours
finds its ideal terrain in dishes such as risotto and fresh ravioli.
I must admit, however, that even a simple cheese toastie with slices
of roasted pumpkin can be extremely satisfying.

PUMPKIN AND YOGHURT

The crisp tartness of yoghurt refreshes and enhances the pumpkin,
mitigating its sometimes cloying sweetness. A spoonful of yoghurt in
a pumpkin soup with a pinch of smoked chilli flakes and chives is an
easy and effective combination.

PUMPKIN AND NUTMEG

Few things excite me like pumpkin ravioli alla mantovana,
featuring a generous dose of nutmeg. This warm and enveloping spice
reveals balsamic and citrus notes when combined with pumpkin flesh.
I would like to specify that the nutmeg should be freshly grated;
ready-ground nutmeg has a somewhat dusty aroma and loses most of
its aromatic nuances.

PUMPKIN AND PANCETTA

The smoky notes of pancetta make it the perfect partner to the
pumpkin, giving a much more interesting and complex result than you
might imagine. A warm salad of roasted pumpkin, crispy pancetta,
chestnuts, onion petals and pickled mustard seeds, has a wonderfully
complete flavour profile.

DELICA SQUASH GNOCCHI,
PECORINO, JERUSALEM ARTICHOKE

Serves 6

There is something extremely comforting and cosy about this combination of ingredients: sweet baked pumpkin, nutmeg and cheese fondue, with the scent of hazelnut butter wafting through. We have added a few other elements to make it more fun and unusual, such as the coffee powder and the crispy Jerusalem artichoke chips. This is the ideal dish for a slow Sunday lunch with friends, when the days are starting to get colder and greyer, and the need to stay at home is kicking in. Make sure you can take a little nap on the couch after the lunch just described; it amplifies the effect.

Ingredients

For the gnocchi
600 g (1 lb 5 oz) Delica squash
6 medium-sized potatoes
2 egg yolks
30 g (1 oz) Parmesan, grated
½ nutmeg, grated
pinch of salt
40 g (1½ oz/⅓ cup) chestnut flour
120 g (4¼ oz/scant 1 cup) '00' flour, plus
    extra for dusting

For the Jerusalem artichoke chips
oil, for deep-frying
4 Jerusalem artichokes, finely sliced
    with a mandoline

To serve
150 g (5 oz) hazelnut butter, infused with sage
coffee powder
100 g (3½ oz) Pecorino Fondue (page 236)

Method

1. Make the gnocchi: Preheat the oven to 210°C fan (410°F).

2. Cut the squash into wedges, remove the seeds and arrange on a baking tray. Wash the potatoes and place on another baking tray. Bake the squash for 20 minutes and the potatoes for 35 minutes.

3. Once cool enough to handle, remove the skins from both. In two separate bowls, mash the potatoes and squash. You will need 300 g (10½ oz) of each.

4. In a large bowl, combine the cooked potato and squash with the egg yolks, Parmesan, grated nutmeg and a good pinch of salt. Add both flours and mix with a spatula until everything is combined.

5. Tip the dough out on to the work surface and knead gently, keeping your hands flat. Be careful not to overwork the dough; it should feel soft and delicate. Shape it into a ball and set aside.

6. Place a clean tea towel on a baking tray and dust with some flour.

7. Lightly flour your work surface. Divide the dough into three equal portions, then take one and roll it out into a rope about 2 cm (¾ in) thick. With a sharp knife, cut it into 2.5 cm (1 in) pieces. Arrange the gnocchi on the prepared tray, making sure they don't touch. Dust with some extra flour if they look too moist.

8. Make the jersulaem artichoke chips: Pour oil into a medium-sized saucepan to a depth of 5 cm (2 in). Place over a medium heat and, when it reaches 170–180°C begin to fry the artichoke slices in batches of a few at a time. Fry for about 5 minutes until golden brown, then use a slotted spoon to lift them out and transfer to a plate lined with paper towels.

9. Repeat with the remaining artichoke slices.

→   Continued on Following Page

10. Cook and assemble: Bring a large pan of salted water to the boil, then add the gnocchi and cook, stirring occasionally, until they float the surface. This should take about 4 minutes, or when they begin to float to the top of the pan. Remove with a slotted spoon and place in a large, warm mixing bowl. Add half of the hazelnut butter and gently move the bowl in circles to combine and achieve a nice glossy sauce.

11. Divide the gnocchi between six warm bowls. Top with more hazelnut butter, then lightly dust with the coffee powder. Drizzle over some Pecorino fondue, then scatter over the with Jerusalem artichoke chips and serve.

Chef's Notes

Storage: If you make more gnocchi than you need, you can freeze them. Arrange them on a tray, well spaced out, then place in the freezer. Once frozen, transfer to a freezer-proof container. Cook them in the same way; there's no need to defrost first, but they will take a few minutes longer.

RED CABBAGE, ORANGE, JUS

Serves 6

Here we play one of our favourite games: taking a vegetable and elevating it to make it the star of the dish, treating it like a highly prized ingredient. The humble and often mistreated red cabbage can, with the right tricks, become silky, meaty and very complex. I invite you to try this game with other vegetables, too; take something simple, change the point of view, and approach it as if it were an expensive steak or a rare fish, devoting time and technique to it. The results can be surprising.

Ingredients

2 small red cabbages (about 700 g/1 lb 9 oz each)
1 litre (34 fl oz/4 cups) freshly pressed orange juice
5 bay leaves
3 garlic cloves
70 g (2¼ oz) Meat Jus (page 236)
olive oil, salt

For the cumin brown butter
18 g (¾ oz/2 tablespoons) cumin seeds
50 g (2 oz) Brown Butter (see page 233)

To serve
orange zest
lemon thyme leaves

Method

1. *Roast and braise the cabbage:* Preheat the oven to 220°C fan (430°F/gas 9).

2. Cut each red cabbage into four wedges. Rub with oil and salt, making sure you get into the layers and do not just season the surface. Place on a baking tray and roast for 15 minutes, turning the wedges halfway through cooking. They should be golden brown with caramelised ends, but not cooked through.

3. Pack the cabbage wedges tightly together in a saucepan. Add the orange juice, bay leaves and garlic. Simmer gently over a low–medium heat for 45 minutes until the cabbage is tender and the cooking juices have reduced. Place the cabbage wedges on a clean baking tray and set aside.

4. *Make the cumin brown butter:* Toast the cumin seeds in a dry frying pan for 2 minutes until fragrant, then pound using a pestle and mortar. Warm the butter and add the cumin. Stir and leave to infuse for 10 minutes.

5. *Assemble:* Preheat the grill (broiler) to high. Grill the cabbage wedges for 5 minutes until hot and caramelised. Brush with the cumin butter and lamb jus, then grill again for another minute.

6. Grate over some fresh orange zest and sprinkle with lemon thyme. Arrange on six warm plates and finish with a final touch of lamb jus.

Chef's Notes

Keep it veggie: We use the lamb jus to emphasise the meatiness of the dish and to reverse the roles of protagonist and seasoning. If you want to keep it veggie, you can opt for the Soy and Wine Glaze on page 236.

Choosing your cabbages: We like to work with small cabbages; the leaves are thinner and more tender. If you can't find any, you can opt for a larger red cabbage, adjusting the cooking time accordingly. This recipe also works very well with other cabbage types, such as savoy, hispi, napa or endives.

MOROSETA

CROAKER, ONION, THYME

Serves 6

The star of this dish, with all due respect to fish, is her majesty the onion. We make a super-concentrated broth: an essence of onion soup, to be precise. We start by browning onions super gently before simmering them in a broth for hours; the scent this gives off is incredible. It is very interesting to make the same broth with different types of onion at different times of the year, noticing the differences. There's the sweetness of leek, the green and pungent character of spring onions, the expressive power of shallots—I could talk about onions for days.

Ingredients

6 small white onions, halved
2 tablespoons olive oil, plus extra to serve
Elderflower Vinegar (page 74)
500 g (1 lb 2 oz) croaker fillet, cut into 6 equal portions
sugar, salt, freshly ground black pepper

For the broth
50 g (2¾ oz) grape seed oil
1.5 kg (3 lb 5 oz) white onions, finely sliced
bunch of thyme, plus extra to serve
300 g (10½ oz) white wine
2 litres (70 fl oz/8 cups) water

Method

1. Make the broth: Heat the grapeseed oil in a large saucepan over a medium-low heat. Add the onions and thyme and cook gently for 30 minutes, until the onions are tender and starting to turn a nice deep caramel colour.

2. Add the wine and cook for a further 10 minutes, allowing the alcohol to evaporate. Pour in the water, increase the heat and bring to the boil.

3. Reduce the heat to low and simmer for 3 hours, then strain the broth through a sieve. Taste and add salt as needed.

4. Make the onion petals: Season each onion half with salt, pepper and a pinch of sugar. Leave to rest for 15 minutes.

5. Heat the olive oil in a large cast-iron pan over a medium heat. Add the onions, placing them cut-sides down. Cook for 8 minutes, then reduce the heat to low and continue cooking for a further 20 minutes. Prick with a skewer to check that all the layers are cooked through. Leave to cool completely.

6. Once cool, starting with the outer layers, divide each onion half into petals. Place on a tray and season lightly with few drops of elderflower vinegar. Taste and adjust the seasoning as needed.

7. Grill the fish: Remove any bones from the fish using fish tweezers. Season with salt, massage on all sides and leave to rest for 10 minutes.

8. Preheat the barbecue to medium heat. Grill the fish skin-side down for about 6 minutes. Check the internal temperature with a thermometer; it should be around 50°C (122°F).

9. Divide the fish between six warm bowls, then add a small ladleful of hot onion broth to each. Arrange the onion petals harmoniously on top, and finish with some thyme leaves and a few drops of olive oil.

Chef's Notes

Broth: The broth is the real protagonist of this dish. You can use it as a base for excellent soups, risotto or ravioli. You can also intensify it by reducing it further or adding reinforcing elements, such as meat jus, fish broth or miso.

Serves 6

The name already suggests the bursting character of this dish. *Bombette* (literally 'small bombs') is an iconic Apulian meat dish: small pork rolls filled with *caciocavallo* cheese and sausage. They are rigorously cooked on the barbecue, spiked on huge metal skewers, and served with no sides or sauces. Our version is quite respectful; we mainly focus on creating an aromatic filling and balancing the flavours with natural acidity of quince, which grows abundantly in our fields from October onwards, and the bitterness of radicchio, gently braised with white wine and anchovies.

Ingredients

500 g (1 lb 2 oz) pork capocollo in very thin silces of about 20 g (¾ oz) each (have it sliced by the butcher)

For the filling
2 tablespoons olive oil
4 shallots, thinly sliced
10 g (½ oz) Warm Spice Blend (page 245)
60 g (2 oz) stale bread
8 g (¼ oz) sage leaves
10 g (½ oz) garlic cloves, grated
80 g (3 oz) Parmesan, grated
200 g (7 oz) Italian sausage
200 g (7 oz) minced pork
10 g (½ oz/2 teaspoons) salt
1 egg

For the sauce:
½ quince, peeled and diced
juice of ½ lemon
15 g (½ oz/generous 1 tablespoon) cane sugar
200 g (7 oz) Meat Jus (page 236)
60 g (2 oz/¼ cup) water

For the radicchio
40 g (1½ oz/3¼ tablespoons) oil
2 garlic cloves
6 anchovy fillets
2 red radicchio treviso, each cut into 4 wedges
200 g (7 oz/scant 1 cup) white wine

To finish
1 radicchio tardivo, leaves separated
60 g (2 oz) toasted hazelnuts

Method

1. **Prepare the filling and bombette:** Heat the olive oil in a saucepan over a medium-low heat. Add the shallots and spice blend, cook for about 12 minutes. Allow to cool, then chop into a paste.

2. In a blender, blend the bread with the sage and garlic, then tip into a bowl. Add the shallot paste and remaining filling ingredients, and stir to combine. It should have the consistency of meatball mix. Cover and leave to rest in the refrigerator for 2 hours.

3. Take one of the meat slices and put about 25 g (1 oz) of filling in the middle. Roll up tightly and repeat with the remaining meat and filling. Once ready, thread on to metal barbecue skewers and set aside.

4. **Make the sauce:** Preheat the oven to 180°C fan (350°F/gas 6).

5. Put the quince into a small bowl. Season with lemon and sugar, then macerate for 15 minutes. Transfer into a small baking dish and bake for 15 minutes until golden brown and starting to soften.

6. Tip the cooked fruit into a saucepan with the meat jus and water. Place over a low heat and simmer gently for half an hour. Pass through a muslin and set aside.

7. **Cook the radicchio:** Heat the oil in a large frying pan over a medium heat. Add the garlic and anchovy and cook until the garlic is golden and the anchovy has completely dissolved. Add the radicchio and cook for 5 minutes, turning to cook both sides.

8. Add the wine and cook for 3 minutes, then reduce the heat to low and simmer for 15 minutes until the liquid has reduced and the radicchio is tender.

9. **Cook the bombette and assemble:** Preheat the barbecue to medium. Cook the bombette for about 12–15 minutes, turning often until evenly browned. Remove from the skewers and keep warm.

10. Arrange a few leaves of radicchio on each plate, then place the bombette on top and glaze with the sauce. Finish with a few tardivo leaves and a scattering of toasted hazelnuts, and serve.

POTATO-SKIN GELATO

<u>Makes 1 kg (2 lb 4 oz)</u>

I don't remember exactly when we started making this, but I remember very well how we got there. We had gnocchi on the menu, so we baked a good amount of whole potatoes in the oven, to dry them out as much as possible. After about 20 minutes, the whole kitchen would be pervaded with a caramel-like smell, reminiscent of toasted hazelnuts and milk chocolate. It was simply the potatoes, cooked without any fat or seasoning, releasing all their caramel essence. From there, it was a short step; we wanted to try and capture that magical scent. Once the flesh was removed, the peels went back into the oven to roast them completely, and then we used them to infuse some milk that would become our first attempt at potato-skin gelato. Later, we also added malt to the base to further emphasise the caramel component.

<u>Ingredients</u>

800 g (1 lb 12 oz) potatoes
680 g (1 lb 8 oz/2¾ cups) milk
150 g (5 oz/⅔ cup) fresh cream
55 g (2 oz) barley malt
80 g (3 oz/⅓ cup) sugar
40 g (1½ oz) honey
4 g (¼ oz) carob seed powder
2 g (1/8 oz) salt, plus an extra pinch to serve

Method

1. Prepare the potato skins: Preheat the oven to 200°C fan (400°F/gas 7).

2. Wash the potatoes, then place on a baking tray and bake for 35–45 minutes until cooked through. Allow to cool slightly, then peel, keeping the flesh for another purpose. You should have about 65 g (2¼ oz) of peel.

3. Arrange the peel on the baking tray and reduce the oven temperature to 180°C fan (350°F/gas 6). Roast them for 10 minutes until golden brown and dry.

4. Make the gelato: In a large saucepan over a low heat, heat the milk to about 60°C (140°F). Take the pan off the heat and add the toasted potato skins, crumbling them coarsely with your hands. Stir well, then cover the pan with a lid and leave to infuse for 2 hours.

5. After 2 hours, strain through a sieve, pressing well to extract as much flavour as possible. Weigh the milk and check that you still have 680 g (1 lb 8 oz /2¾ cups); it may have decreased considerably, as the potato skins may have absorbed some liquid. Top up any missing milk, then pour into a clean saucepan and add the cream and malt.

6. Cook over a low–medium heat until it reaches 40°C (104°F), then add the other ingredients. Continue cooking until the mixture reaches 85°C (185°F), stirring often. Take the pan off the heat and blend with an immersion blender for a few seconds, then transfer into a container with a lid. Cool quickly with in an ice bath.

7. Once cold, chill in the refrigerator for 12 hours.

8. The following day, you will notice that the mixture is thicker and a little elastic. Blend for a few seconds and then add to your gelato machine and churn according to the manufacturer's instructions. Serve with an extra pinch of salt.

PEARS, SAFFRON, HONEY

Serves 6

The world is divided into those who love cooked fruit and those who consider it hospital food. In my kitchen, cooked fruit reigns supreme; regardless of the season, there is always a good reason to poach, bake or roast fruits.

Poached pears are a classic, the perfect end to an autumn meal: elegant, fresh, mouthwatering, and not too heavy. Perhaps the most difficult part is finding suitable pears. They must be firm, ripe to the right point, medium in size and with smooth, non-grainy flesh.

Ingredients

1 litre (34 fl oz/4 cups) water
zest and juice of 1 lemon
200 g (7 oz/scant 1 cup) sugar
pinch of saffron strands
3 g (⅛ oz) timut peppercorns
6 medium-sized, firm and fairly ripe pears,
    peeled but left whole
120 g (4¼ oz/generous ⅓ cup) honey
2 lemon leaves

Method

1. In a deep saucepan, combine the water, lemon zest and juice and sugar to make a syrup. Cook for 10 minutes over a low heat.

2. In a small bowl or cup, rehydrate the saffron strands in a spoonful of the lukewarm syrup. Leave to infuse for 5 minutes.

3. Meanwhile, toast the peppercorns in a dry frying pan over a medium heat for a couple of minutes until fragrant.

4. Add the pears to the syrup, along with the saffron infusion and toasted peppercorns. Make a cartouche and place it on the surface. This will allow partial evaporation and, most importantly, it will keep the pears submerged in their liquid. Bring gently to the boil and simmer for 15 minutes.

5. Check the consistency of the pears with a skewer; they should be cooked but still firm, and begin to have a shiny appearance. Once they've reached this stage, turn off the heat and leave to cool in their syrup.

6. Serve at room temperature with a little of their poaching liquid.

Chef's Notes

Pairings: These pears are perfect served with a whipped ricotta cream (see page 43) and some butter biscuits.

Storage: The pears will keep well in their syrup for up to 3 days, stored in the refrigerator. The longer they rest, the more they will soften.

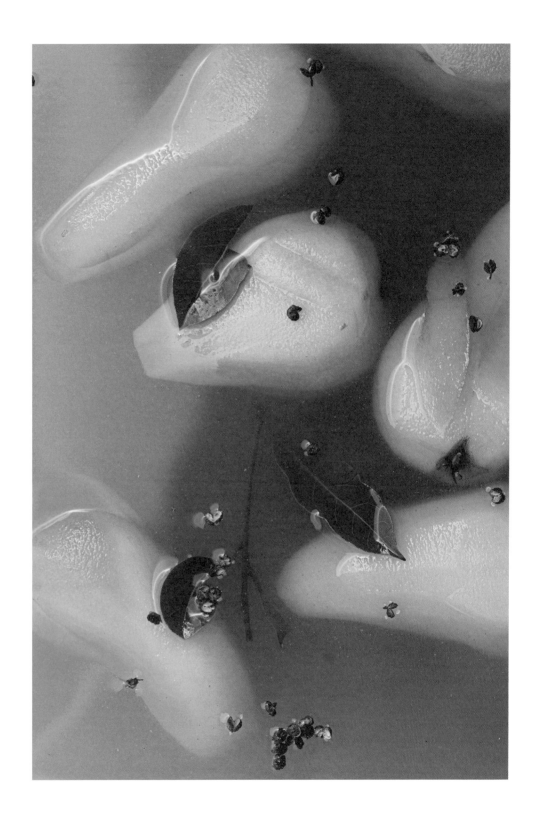

MOROSETA

MOROSETA

SBRISOLONA WITH POLENTA, HAZELNUT, TANGERINE

Serves 8

Sbrisolona is a typical recipe from northern Italy: a crumbly cake consisting of crunchy bits made with polenta flour, sugar, lard and butter, and covered with nuts. It has a simple and convivial nature, and is traditionally served in large pieces to be shared with other diners, dipped in cream or paired with a glass of sweet wine. Our version is slightly different; it includes semolina flour, tangerine zest and a good dose of salt. The crispy texture and buttery, salty flavour make it decidedly addictive.

Ingredients

250 g (9 oz) cold butter
100 g (3½ oz/1 cup) almond flour
150 g (5 oz/scant 1⅓ cups) hazelnut flour
100 g (3½ oz/generous ¾ cup) spelt flour
100 g (3½ oz/⅔ cup) polenta flour
100 g (3½ oz/generous ¾ cup) semolina flour
250 g (9 oz/1⅓ cups) brown sugar
10 g (½ oz/2 teaspoons) sea salt flakes,
    plus extra for sprinkling
zest of 3 tangerines
100 g (3½ oz/¾ cup) hazelnuts

Method

1. Mix: Toast the polenta flour in a dry frying pan over a low–medium heat for at least 5 minutes, stirring often. It should turn dark yellow and smell deliciously toasted. Spread out on a tray and leave to cool.

2. Once cool, tip into a large bowl, along with all the other ingredients. Work it all together with your fingertips until coarse crumbs form. Tip into a container, cover and leave in the refrigerator for at least 6 hours.

3. Bake: Preheat the oven to 170°C fan (340°F/gas 5) and line a 28 cm (11 in) cake tin with baking parchment.

4. Evenly spread out the crumbs in the prepared tin; the mixture should be about 2.5 cm (1 in) deep. Press it lightly with damp hands; the water will help the crumbs to stick together. Sprinkle a pinch of salt over the surface and bake for 20–25 minutes until nicely browned (its deliciousness lies in this toasted finish).

5. Leave to cool on a cooling rack before serving.

APPLE, SPELT
AND CORIANDER CAKE

Serves 6–8

It may be a cliché, but few things say 'autumn' quite like an apple cake for *merènda* (an afternoon snack). This version is very much to my personal taste: spelt flour and almonds give it a bit of a rustic flavour, the apples are marinated in lemon for an extra kick of acidity, which is enhanced by the sour cream, and the coriander seeds give it a nice aroma that goes surprisingly well with the apples.

It looks simple, very grandma-like, but the taste reveals an unexpected character that makes it unique – it's very different from other apple cake recipes. For extra indulgence, I recommend serving with a scoop of gelato or some whipped cream.

Ingredients

170 g (6 oz) butter, at room temperature,
    plus extra for greasing
1 teaspoon coriander seeds
3 small apples
juice of ½ lemon
125 g (4 oz/generous ½ cup) cane sugar
50 g (2 oz/2½ tablespoons) coriander honey
    (or other honey of your choice)
2 g (⅛ oz) salt
2 large eggs
60 g (2 oz/¼ cup) sour cream
100 g (3½ oz/generous ¾ cup) plain (all-purpose) flour
75 g (2½ oz/generous ½ cup) spelt flour
2 teaspoons baking powder
125 g (4 oz/1¼ cups) almond flour
icing (powdered) sugar, to dust

For the glaze
25 g (1 oz/1¼ tablespoons) honey, preferably coriander
20 g (¾ oz/1½ tablespoons) lemon juice

Method

1. **Mix the cake batter:** Preheat the oven to 170°C fan (340°F/gas 5). Lightly grease a 24 cm (9 ½ in) cake tin and line with baking parchment, making the parchment stick well.

2. In a dry frying pan over a medium heat, toast the coriander seeds for 2 minutes until fragrant, then crush with a pestle and mortar. Set aside.

3. Peel two of the apples and cut them into small dice. Tip into a bowl and marinate with the lemon juice.

4. In a stand mixer fitted with the paddle attachment, combine the butter, sugar, honey, ground coriander seeds and salt. Mix at medium speed for a few minutes until the mixture is light and fluffy (the sugar should be almost invisible). Gradually incorporate the eggs and sour cream at a low speed, making sure every addition is absorbed before adding more.

5. Sift the flours into a separate bowl, along with the baking powder. Using a spatula, start adding the almond flour to the mixer, followed by the sifted flour mix, adding a little at a time and mixing between each addition until fully combined.

6. **Bake and glaze:** Divide the cake batter into two separate bowls. Add the marinated apple cubes to one of these bowls, draining away any juice that may have formed. Pour this mixture into the prepared baking tin, and level out with a spatula, then pour in the second bowl of batter.

7. Cut the remaining apple into slices and distribute them evenly over the surface.

8. Bake for about 35 minutes until golden and fragrant. To check it's done, insert a skewer into the centre of the cake; it should come out dry and clean.

9. To make the glaze, gently warm the honey and lemon juice in a small saucepan over a low heat. Brush generously over the surface of the cake and allow to cool on a cooling rack before serving with a dusting of icing sugar.

SMOKED QUINCE
AND FIVE-SPICE SHRUB

Makes about 2 litres (75 fl oz)

We have a somewhat controversial relationship with
quinces. Their delicate flavour is directly proportional
to the gigantic amount of work that goes into preparing
them, especially when it comes to the quinces that grow
undisturbed and practically wild in the fields around
Moroseta. They are the favourite snack of worms and
insects, which have to be removed one by one – a very
long and difficult job, given the particular hardness of
the fruit pulp. In the case of this shrub, however, you can
rest assured that the preparation is easy; the quince
does not even have to be peeled.

The smoky and spicy components used here make this
shrub very complex. It's particularly good as an aperitif
in the cold season, vaguely reminiscent of a good whisky.

Ingredients

1 kg (2 lb 4 oz) quinces
5 g (¼ oz) long peppercorns
10 g (½ oz) coriander seeds
600 g (1 lb 5 oz/generous 2½ cups) cane sugar
1.2 litres (40 fl oz/4¾ cups) water
1 cinnamon stick
zest and juice of 3 bergamots
380 ml (13 ½ oz/scant 1½ cups) unpasteurised
    apple cider vinegar

Method

1. Smoke the quinces for about 20 minutes in a
    kamado oven or barbecue. They don't need to
    be cooked; we just want that smoky aroma.
    Roughly chop them, leaving both skin and core.

2. Toast the peppercorns and coriander seeds in a
    dry frying pan over a medium heat for 2 minutes
    until fragrant.

3. In a medium saucepan, combine the smoked
    quinces with the sugar, water, toasted spices,
    cinnamon stick and bergamot zest. Bring to the
    boil, then reduce the heat to low and simmer
    very gently for one hour. If the water reduces
    too much, add a little more.

4. Pour into a container and add the bergamot juice.
    Mix well and leave to rest at room temperature
    for 24 hours.

5. The next day, add the vinegar and leave to
    macerate for a couple of days.

6. Strain through a sieve and transfer the strained
    liquid into a sterilised glass bottle. This will keep
    in the refrigerator up to 3 months.

04 WINTER

In winter, the masseria becomes suspended in time; the rhythms are dilated, the bright winter light pervades all the rooms, there is a unique sense of tranquility. I have always appreciated this great difference between the different times of the year – it is as if we were following nature's course. In winter we devote ourselves more to cooking classes or workshops, the kitchen dabbles in carefully prepared menus for a few guests, looking forward to the not-too-distant holidays. We also have a good number of returning guests who come just as if they were visiting friends at Christmas time. It's an opportunity for us to relax, to sit at our own table.

Winter food is of course hearty and comforting, with familiar foods such as fresh pasta, legumes, copious amounts of butter and citrus fruits all making an appearance.

FRIED EGGS, TOAST, KIMCHI BUTTER

Serves 6

In winter, it becomes more difficult to get up, especially for the fellows who have the breakfast shift. It takes a lot of motivation to get to work when it is still dark, the kitchen is cold and the vegetable garden is covered by a blanket of fog (that's right, there is fog in Puglia too). This toast was born as a motivational treat for the brave staff who carry on the breakfast shift with tenacity and pride, even in the harshest months. We used to eat it standing at the steel counter in the kitchen, before the customers' orders arrived, but the result was so convincing in its absolute simplicity, that after a few weeks, it made its way on to the menu, meeting with unexpected success there too.

Ingredients

40 g (1½ oz) kimchi, finely chopped
120 g (4¼ oz) butter, at room temperature
1 teaspoon smoked chilli flakes
6 thick slices of Olive Oil Pan Brioche (page 239)
50 g (2 oz) olive oil
6 eggs
small handful of wild rocket leaves
vinegar, for drizzling
salt and freshly ground black pepper

Method

1. Make the kimchi butter: If the kimchi is very wet, blot it with paper towels.

2. In a bowl, combine the room-temperature butter with the chopped kimchi, chilli flakes and a good pinch of salt (if the kimchi is very savoury and/or spicy, you can omit the salt or the chilli flakes, or balance it with some honey). Mix well to combine.

3. Toast the brioche: Preheat the grill to 210°C (410°F) and toast the brioche slices for 5 minutes until they are golden brown but still soft inside. Let cool for a few minutes on a wire rack.

4. Fry the eggs and assemble: Meanwhile, heat a non-stick frying pan over a medium heat, and add a little oil – just enough to cover the entire surface of the pan. Once the oil is hot, crack in the eggs. I recommend cooking a maximum of three at a time, especially if you want crispy, well-defined edges. Season each egg with salt and pepper, and cook for 4 minutes. The yolks should remain glossy and runny.

5. Generously spread the bread slices with the kimchi butter, and place a fried egg on top of each one. Season the greens with a drop of vinegar and garnish the eggs and rocket then serve immediately.

Chef's Notes

Tasty additions: Try adding cheese (a cloud of Parmesan on the hot egg goes very well), some fried bacon or pancetta, or anchovies, of course.

MOROSETA

WINTER GIARDINIERA

Makes a 2 litre (70 fl oz/8 cup) jar

Winter garden produce is particularly good for pickling, as its crispness and firmness hold up well. We make large jars of these pickles from mid-November onwards, using whatever is available in the garden. The first jars of the season are more delicate and colourful, with the batches becoming more monochromatic as time goes on, consisting mainly of roots such as kohlrabi, daikon and celeriac. These pickles are the perfect accompaniment to pâtés, cheeses and terrines, giving that absolutely irresistible crunchy acidic counterpoint.

Ingredients

4 red onions (they tend to release their colour,
    so if you want each vegetable to retain its natural
    colour, opt for a white onion)
1 bunch of radishes
3 celery stalks
2 small fennel bulbs
1 small cauliflower
3 small carrots

For the aromatics
8 bay leaves
5 g (¼ oz) black pepper
4 garlic cloves, peeled and halved lengthways
2 juniper berries

For the pickling liquid
900 ml (30½ fl oz/generous 3½ cups) water
540 ml (18¼ fl oz/generous 2 cups) white wine vinegar
320 g (10¾ oz/1⅓ cups) sugar

Method

1. Prepare the vegetables: Wash and clean the vegetables. The radishes can be left whole or cut in half, depending on size. Cut the celery into 5 cm (2 in) portions, peeling it with a potato peeler if it is particularly fibrous. Cut the fennel into 6 wedges, keeping the base intact. Divide the cauliflower into florets, and chop the stem into 2 cm (¾ in) chunks. There's no need to peel the carrots; just scrape them well with a vegetable brush to remove any soil, then either halve them lengthways or slice diagonally into 2 cm (¾ in) slices.

2. Arrange all the cut vegetables in a sterilised jar, then tuck the aromatics in amongst them.

3. Prepare the pickling liquid and seal: In a large saucepan over a low heat, combine the ingredients for the pickling liquid and heat until the sugar has dissolved. Carefully pour this liquid into the vegetable jar and seal tightly.

4. Place the sealed jar in a pan of cold water, making sure the water reaches past the lid. Bring to the boil, then simmer for 15 minutes. Take off the heat allow to cool completely in the pan.

5. Leave to pickle for at least 3 weeks before consuming.

RABBIT RILLETTES

Serves 6–8

Although it is delicious, rabbit is not an easy meat; its delicate flesh has a tendency to dry out easily, and can become stodgy. It is even more complicated to serve it to many guests at the same time, as it has very different parts and is full of tricky little bones. To solve this problem and satisfy my desire to serve rabbit, we started studying a classic French dish, rillettes, but combined it with the idea of Italian-style braised rabbit, sensibly reducing the amount of fat and playing with vaguely medieval flavours and aromas. The result is enveloping and creamy, perfect for spreading on bread, and makes the ideal accompaniment to pickles, some salad and a good glass of wine.

Ingredients

1 rabbit, about 2 kg (4 lb 8 oz), jointed

For the brine
2 litres (70 fl oz/8 cups) water
200 g (7 oz/scant 1 cup) muscovado sugar
200 g (7 oz/scant 1 cup) salt
10 bay leaves
5 g (¼ oz) black pepper
1 garlic bulb

For braising
200 g (7 oz) pork fat
80 g (3 oz) grapeseed oil
750 ml (25 fl oz/3 cups) dry rosé wine
2 cardamom pods
6 g (¼ oz) juniper berries
3 g (1/8 oz) cloves
11 g (½ oz) long peppercorns

For the second cooking
100 g (3½ oz) pork fat
4 carrots, finely diced
2 small onions, finely diced

To serve
Winter Giardinera (page 187)
mustard
toast

Method

1. Brine the rabbit: Combine the water, sugar and salt in a large saucepan over a medium heat and bring to a light boil. Take off the heat and pour into a container that will be large enough to hold the rabbit. Add the bay leaves, pepper and garlic and leave to cool to room temperature.

2. Once cool, add the rabbit pieces, making sure the meat is well submerged in the liquid, then transfer to the refrigerator and leave for 12 hours or overnight.

3. Braise the rabbit: The next day, remove the rabbit pieces from the brine and pat well with paper towels. Leave to air-dry for at least 30 minutes.

4. Heat the pork fat and oil in a large, deep saucepan over a medium heat. Add the rabbit pieces and brown on all sides for 5–6 minutes, until golden brown. Add the wine and aromatics. Allow the alcohol to evaporate for about 2 minutes, then reduce the heat to low and braise gently for 2 hours, until the meat is tender but not falling apart.

5. After 2 hours, remove the rabbit from the pan and leave to cool on a large plate for 15 minutes, then allow to cool a little and debone with your hands.

6. Pour the cooking juices into a blender and blend to combine, then pass through a fine sieve.

7. Make the rillettes: Return the now-empty pan to a medium heat. Add the second amount of pork fat and, once melted, add the carrots and onions. Cook for 15 minutes, until well browned, then add the boneless cooked rabbit and the strained jus. Reduce the heat to low and cook for 30 minutes.

8. Transfer into a container and cover the surface with baking parchment. Leave to cool, then transfer to the refrigerator for at least 1 day to stabilise.

9. Serve: The following day, remove the layer of fat that will have formed on its surface. Let the rillettes come up to room temperature, then serve with pickles, mustard and toast. If you wish, it can be whipped to be soft and light.

KABOCHA SQUASH SOUP,
'NDUJA RED PRAWNS

Serves 6

A small bowl of soup, served halfway through the tasting menu, delights and nourishes, setting the right mood for the courses to follow.

Squash soup, clichéd as it may sound, is one of the dishes we make most often, constantly renewing aromas and combinations; it is a bit like our winter equivalent of gazpacho. Its natural sweetness gives us an excellent base from which to experiment, playing with contrasts, acidity and spiciness. This version is a concentration of flavours that I particularly like: the base is spiced with a little black cardamom and mint, and made even creamier by the almond milk, which in turn welcomes the delicious silkiness of local red prawns and spiciness of Calabrian 'nduja.

Ingredients

1 kabocha squash, about 2 kg (4 lb 8 oz)
80 g (3 oz) olive oil
3 black cardamom pods
1 onion, finely sliced
2 shallots, finely sliced
3 mint sprigs
500 ml (17 fl oz/2 cups) unsweetened almond milk
about 400 g (14 oz/1¾ cups) water
juice of ½ lime
salt flakes

For the prawns
18 red prawns (shrimp)
few drops of olive oil
zest of 1 orange

To serve
'Nduja Oil (page 244)
pinch of sumac
bronze fennel fronds

Method

1. Roast the squash: Preheat the oven to 210°C fan (410°F/gas 8).

2. Peel and deseed the squash, then chop the flesh into 3 cm (1¼ in) chunks; you should have about 900 g (2 lb) of prepared squash. Spread out the squash chunks on a baking tray. Drizzle over half of the oil and season with salt. Roast for 20 minutes until golden brown.

3. Prepare the prawns: Meanwhile, clean the prawns by removing the heads, shells and dark guts. Arrange neatly and keep chilled until ready to serve.

4. Make the soup: Toast the whole cardamom pods in a dry frying pan over a medium heat for a few minutes until fragrant. Set aside.

5. Heat the remaining oil in a large saucepan over a medium heat. Add the onion and shallot, and cook gently for 15 minutes until translucent. Add the roasted squash, cardamom pods and mint sprigs, and cook for a few minutes to let all the flavours get familiar.

6. Add the almond milk and water; you need enough water to cover the ingredients. Bring to the boil, then reduce the heat to low and simmer for 30 minutes.

7. Remove the cardamom and mint, then transfer the soup into a blender. Add the lime juice and blend at maximum power for 2 minutes until smooth and glossy. Usually it is not necessary to pass this soup through a sieve, but if it looks a bit grainy, you can do so. Taste, adjust the salt and set aside.

8. Assemble: When you're ready to serve, let the prawns sit at room temperature for a few minutes so they are not too cold.

9. Season them with freshly grated orange peel, timut pepper, flaked salt and a few drops of oil, making sure you distribute the flavours evenly.

10. Divide the soup between six warm bowls and arrange three prawns in each. Garnish with a few drops of 'nduja oil (depending on how spicy you like it), a pinch of sumac and some fennel fronds.

ON ARTICHOKE

Every season has its king, and the artichoke reigns supreme in the winter months. Its extreme versatility and its taste – somewhere between bitter, herbaceous and sweet – make it irresistible to me. My Roman origins probably also come into play in this; I can eat huge quantities of artichokes for days, without ever getting bored.

The artichoke's season is extensive, starting in November and lasting all the way into early spring. There are many varieties and sizes, from the prickly, insidious Sardinian artichokes to the majestic Roman Mammole, via the tiny ones we preserve in oil. Each has its own distinctive note. In the kitchen, we work a lot with local varieties, particularly the Brindisi Violet, a delicious native variety with an ancient flavour pushed to the bitter side, masterfully recovered by our trusted farmer Antonio.

The artichoke's combination of complexity, nobility and meatiness means it is a perfect vegetable protagonist, able to stand up to important sauces and significant richness, becoming as interesting as fine cuts of meat or fish. Not only does it taste incredible, but there is also something magical about its texture: compact and yielding at the same time, with a firm, chewy exterior and a velvety core.

The basic tools you'll need for the cleaning process are a vegetable peeler, a small serrated knife, a melon baller (to remove any internal fuzzy choke), and a large bowl of acidulated cold water to keep the freshly cleaned artichokes from oxidising. The process requires care, but after a little practice, you will find it easy to reach the tender heart of this ancient vegetable in just a few steps.

ARTICHOKE AND FRESH CHEESE

Fresh cheeses, such as ricotta and Robiola, can be an excellent
base for braised artichokes, perhaps paired with some salsa verde
and nuts for crunchiness. Explore this combination as a starter,
or turn it into a delicious bruschetta.

ARTICHOKE AND HONEY

The typical bitter note of the artichoke goes very well with
honey. Try a light honey glaze at the end of cooking, or make a
honey vinaigrette to dress a salad of raw artichokes, along with
slivers of mature cheese. I find it particularly interesting to use
chestnut honey for an overlay of different levels and nuances of
sweet bitterness.

ARTICHOKE AND BOTTARGA

Bottarga is savoury and marine, with a bitter aftertaste that
becomes even more interesting when combined with artichoke.
Together, they make a winning combination for primi, such as
pasta or risotto, but bottarga is also delightful simply grated
over an artichoke and potato salad. Other types of roe also work
well for the same reason, from the noble and expensive caviar to
the popular Greek taramasalata.

ARTICHOKE AND GARLIC

Perhaps my favourite combination. I simply cannot conceive of how
you can cook an artichoke without also involving a couple of cloves
of garlic. One of the dishes I always like to propose when artichokes
are at their peak is braised artichoke, bagna cauda and some toasted
breadcrumbs, dressed with garlic, parsley and anchovies.

MOROSETA

ARTICHOKE, CHESTNUTS , ALMOND EMULSION

Serves 6

Our local area is particularly devoted to artichokes; there are entire fields dedicated solely to their cultivation. Our farmer Antonio, who is as much in love with this noble and delicious vegetable as we are, has admirably recovered an ancient cultivar that had disappeared for a few years, the Brindisi Violet. Indigenous to our area, it is small, compact and particularly delicious.

Manu is a true master of artichoke cooking, and his way of preparing artichoke has been with us for many years, becoming a classic in our kitchen and never ceasing to delight us. It involves first braising the artichoke in the Roman style, then resting it for a few hours, before finally grilling it to create a crispy, golden wrapper.

Ingredients

juice of 1 lemon
6 medium-sized artichokes
35 g (1⅓ oz) olive oil, plus extra for brushing
4 garlic cloves, peeled and halved
150 g (5 oz) white wine
2 sprigs each thyme and mint
salt

For the chestnuts
20 chestnuts
30 g (1 oz) Garlic Brown Butter (page 233)

To finish
240 g (8½ oz) Almond Emulsion (page 232)
handful of leaves, such as rocket, mizuna or nasturtium
Garlic Citronette (page 234)

Method

1. Prepare the artichokes: Fill a large bowl with water and add the lemon juice, ready to hold the artichokes once prepared.

2. Take the first artichoke and remove the outer leaves until you reach the tenderest core, then trim them off by removing the uppermost part. Shorten the stem to about 5 cm (2 in) from the base and peel it to remove the outer fibres, then round the base using a paring knife or peeler to remove the remains of the leaves.

3. Spread the leaves to see if there is an inner beard, in which case remove it with a small melon baller. Repeat with the remaining artichokes and set aside in the lemon water.

4. Braise the artichokes: Find a saucepan large enough to hold the artichokes upright. Place it over a medium heat and add the oil; it should be enough oil to lightly cover the base. Add the garlic cloves, and let them brown for 3 minutes.

5. Remove the artichokes from the lemon water, making sure they're well drained, then add them to the pan, arranging them upside down. Salt generously and let the artichokes sizzle for 5 minutes until their bottoms are nicely golden.

6. Deglaze the pan with the white wine, until all of the alcohol has evaporated, then reduce the heat to low and cover the pan with a lid. Cook for about 20 minutes, then check if the artichokes are cooked by piercing the base of one with a toothpick; it should be tender but still firm. Transfer the artichokes to a small container, cover with the thyme sprigs and mint, and cover with a lid. Set aside in the refrigerator for a couple of hours.

7. Prepare the chestnuts: Carve each chestnut with a horizontal cut of about 3 cm (1¼ in). Roast the chestnuts over embers or with a blowtorch for 1 minute, until they are browned and the skin begins to blister. Peel the chestnuts, removing the skin and the thin membrane.

→   Continued on Following Page

8. Crumble the nuts coarsely with your hands, then place them in a small bowl and season with the brown butter and a pinch of salt.

9. Finish and assemble: Preheat the oven to 220°C fan (430°F/gas 9).

10. Spread out the chestnuts on a baking tray and toast for a couple of minutes in the oven, to warm them up and release the aroma. Set aside.

11. Preheat the grill (broiler) to medium. Brush the artichokes with oil and arrange them on a baking tray. Place under the grill for 6 minutes until golden and crispy.

12. Meanwhile, take out six plates and spoon a dollop of ajo blanco on to each one, flattening it slightly with the back of the spoon. In a bowl, combine the leaves with the citronette to season. Lay the artichokes on top of the Almond Emulsion, then garnish with the roasted chestnuts and the seasoned leaves. Serve immediately.

CAULIFLOWER SOUP,
EGG YOLK, BUCKWHEAT

Serves 6

We are so in love with this soup that we have even served it for breakfast. It was the last course of an event we did playing on the concept of the morning meal, trying to make it an experience with the same importance as lunch or dinner. We started with a classic bread, butter and jam, before gradually arriving at this soup, enriched with egg yolk and buckwheat – and it was very much appreciated. It proves that ingredients do not have to be confined to certain categories; everything, if used with awareness, can be utilised across the board.

Ingredients

1 medium cauliflower, leaves removed
olive oil, for drizzling
6 g (¼ oz) rice vinegar, plus a few drops for the soup
6 g (¼ oz) Garlic Oil (page 244)
pinch of sugar
90 g (3 ¼ oz) butter
500 g (1 lb 2 oz/2 cups) goat's milk
10 g (½ oz/2 teaspoons) sesame oil
6 eggs
60 g (2 oz/⅓ cup) buckwheat groats
lemon thyme, to garnish
1 onion
salt and freshly ground black pepper

Method

1. Prepare the cauliflower garnishes: Preheat the oven to 210°C fan (410°F/gas 8).

2. Divide the cauliflower into florets and keep the stalk aside. Weigh out 500 g (1 lb 2 oz) of the florets and set aside for the soup. Place the rest of the florets on the baking tray and drizzle with oil, then season with salt and pepper. Roast for 12 minutes, until browned but still firm, then set aside.

3. Meanwhile, peel the outside of the stalk to get to the tender core. Cut this into regular cubes of about 3 mm (⅛ in). Season with the rice vinegar, garlic oil, sugar and a pinch of salt. Mix well and leave to stand for 20 minutes.

4. Make the soup: melt the butter in a medium saucepan over a low–medium heat. Add the reserved cauliflower florets and a good pinch of salt, and cook for 10 minutes until golden brown. Pour in the goat's milk (you may need to add a little more milk or some water if the cauliflower is not covered), and reduce the heat to low. Cook for 35 minutes until the florets are very soft and the milk is well reduced.

5. Transfer into a blender and add the sesame oil and a few drops of rice vinegar. Blend at maximum speed for 2 minutes, then taste and adjust the salt if necessary.

6. Assemble: Divide the warm soup between six warm bowls, allowing a generous ladleful per person.

7. Crack the eggs into another bowl and separate the yolks, using your hands to remove any strands of egg white attached. Place a yolk in the centre of each bowl of soup and season with a pinch of salt. Garnish all around with the roasted cauliflower florets and marinated stalks. Finish with the toasted buckwheat and lemon thyme, and some freshly ground black pepper.

CITRUS SALAD

Serves 6

The salads in this book all have a bit of the same concept: great ingredients, well seasoned, and little else. It's not necessary to add other elements. I like the brutality of a great raw ingredient, in all its expressiveness.

In this case, the protagonist is the colourful variety of citrus fruits that grow proudly in our garden; it is interesting to note the nuances of acidity, bitterness and sweetness that characterise them. Segmenting citrus can be tedious, but the palatal sensation of a silky segment melting in the mouth is hard to beat.

Ingredients

2 oranges
1 blood orange
1 yellow grapefruit
1 pink grapefruit
5 kumquats
pinch of sugar
1 lemon
salt, salt flakes

For the dressing
20 g (¾ oz) Spicy Honey (page 237)
12 g (½ oz) Fennel Flower Vinegar (page 74)
90 ml (3 fl oz/⅓ cup) extra virgin olive oil

To finish
broccoli and turnip greens flowers
bronze fennel fronds

Method

1. Segment the fruits: Segment all the citrus fruits, except the kumquats.

2. To do this, remove the top and bottom of each fruit, so that they rest well on the cutting board. With a sharp knife, remove the peel, starting from the top and following the circular shape of the fruit. Take care to also remove the white pith, which is bitter and particularly difficult to digest.

3. Holding the citrus fruit over a bowl to collect the juice, cut it into segments by inserting the knife between the white membranes of the fruit. It may seem complicated at first, but the fruit already gives us a pattern to follow, and with a little practice it becomes easier. Repeat with the rest.

4. Place the citrus segments in a container, cover with a little of the juice to keep them moist (save the rest for the dressing), and keep refrigerated until ready to use.

5. For the kumquats, simply remove any seeds and season with a pinch of salt and sugar. Massage well and leave to marinate for 15 minutes.

6. Make the dressing: Pour the reserved citrus juice into a saucepan over a medium heat, and heat until reduced by about one third.

7. Pour this into a bowl, then add the honey and vinegar. Add a generous pinch of salt and stir to dissolve. Slowly add the extra virgin olive oil, emulsifying with a whisk.

8. Assemble: Arrange the citrus fruit segments in six chilled, shallow bowls, making sure to alternate the different types. Just before serving, season generously with the honey dressing. Top with the fresh herbs and marinated kumquat slices, and finish with a pinch of flaky salt.

Serves 6

Here I must make an admission of guilt: after pages in which I celebrate our incredible luck in having a vegetable garden, and the importance of selecting local and seasonal ingredients, in this recipe you will find coconut milk. Yes, I know what you are thinking. I had a discussion with my sous chef Manu about this recipe while we were rewriting the notes we took in the kitchen, and after much deliberation, we both agreed that we would rather be honest and tell you openly that while we rarely transgress and buy ingredients that do not perfectly align with our vision, we simply love the way it works – and it's hard to say no, sometimes.

For our part, we can assure you that coconut combined with earthy chickpeas, pasta and that final counterpoint of spices is absolutely irresistible.

Ingredients

240 g (8½ oz) ditali rigati (or other small pasta)
Bay Leaf Oil (page 243)
Spicy Oil (page 244)
fresh marjoram
freshly ground black pepper

For the chickpeas
500 g (1 lb 2 oz/2¼ cups) dried chickpeas
3 litres (104 fl oz/12 cups) water
1 carrot, roughly chopped
2 onions, roughly chopped
2 celery stalks, roughly chopped
1 sweet chilli pepper
4 bay leaves
10 g (½ oz/2 teaspoons) salt
½ teaspoon bicarbonate of soda (baking soda)

For the sauce
30 g (2 oz) olive oil
2 onions, finely chopped
5 g (¼ oz/1 teaspoon) madras curry powder
125 g (4 oz/½ cup) white wine
450 g (1 lb/1¾ cups) Vegetable Broth (page 243)
185 g (6½ oz/generous ¾ cup) Fish Broth (page 241)
200 ml (7 fl oz/scant 1 cup) coconut milk

Method

1. Cook the chickpeas: Soak the chickpeas in a large bowl of water at room temperature for 6–12 hours, changing the water once.

2. Once the soaking time has elapsed, drain, then place them in a large saucepan with the measured water, along with the carrot, onions, celery, bay leaves, chilli, bicarbonate of soda and salt.

3. Slowly bring to the boil and cook very gently until tender; this will take 2–3 hours, depending on the chickpeas. A white foam will form on the surface; remove it with a slotted spoon every half hour and discard. Once ready, leave the chickpeas to cool in their own cooking liquid.

4. Make the sauce: Heat the oil in a medium-sized saucepan over a medium heat. Add the onions and cook for 8–10 minutes until they are translucent and lightly browned, then add the curry powder and cook for 3 minutes so it releases all the flavours.

5. Drain the cooked chickpeas and measure out 500 g (1 lb 2 oz). Set these aside, then add the rest to the pan and cook for 5 minutes to allow them to take on the flavour of the spices. Deglaze the pan with white wine and cook for another 2 minutes to allow the alcohol to evaporate. Add the Vegetable Broth, Fish Broth and coconut milk, and simmer gently for 1½ hours.

6. Transfer to a blender and blend until smooth. Taste and adjust the salt as needed. The sauce should be quite liquid; if it is too thick, add some more Vegetable Broth.

7. Add the reserved 500 g (1 lb 2 oz) whole chickpeas; their texture will contrast with the silky sauce.

8. Cook the pasta and assemble: Cook the pasta in a large pan of boiling salted water to al dente. Drain and add to the chickpea base. Cook for 2 minutes, then turn off the heat and allow to rest for 3 minutes before serving.

9. Divide between six warm bowls and garnish with a few drops of spicy and bay leaf oils, a scattering of freshly ground pepper and some marjoram.

SMOKED POTATO PLIN,
SAFFRON BEURRE BLANC

Serves 6 (8 ravioli per person)

Fresh filled pasta is always a favourite on our menus, but in winter it becomes a constant feature. Compared to our classic tiny tortellini in broth, this ravioli is more indulgent, with a very seductive and silky butter and saffron sauce. The filling is simple and humble: potatoes cooked under ash and lightly smoked, with a good dose of mint and Parmesan, a nod to Sardinian *culurgiones*, Carlo's favourite dish. All in all, it's perfect for a foggy winter evening.

Saffron is a spice that is particularly dear to me, perhaps because in my childhood I used to eat saffron risotto at least twice a week, and for some years now it has also been produced in Puglia with glorious results.

Ingredients

For the pasta
200 g (7 oz/scant 12/3 cups) '00' flour
50 g (2 oz/scant ½ cup) semolina
3 g (1/8 oz/1/2 teaspoon) salt
1 small egg (about 40 g/1½ oz)
7 yolks (about 140 g/4¾ oz)
10 g (½ oz/2 teaspoons) olive oil

For the filling
3 medium-sized potatoes, cooked under ash
    (see notes)
6 g (¼ oz) mint leaves, finely sliced
120 g (4¼ oz) Parmesan cheese, grated
1 egg yolk
salt and ground white pepper

For the sauce
180 g (6½ oz) Saffron Beurre Blanc (page 232)

Method

1. Make the pasta dough: Mix the flour and semolina in the bowl of a stand mixer and add the salt. In a jug, beat together the egg, egg yolks and oil. Slowly add the liquids to the dry ingredients and knead on a medium speed for 7–10 minutes. The dough should be elastic and perfectly combined. Cover with cling film (plastic wrap) and leave to rest for at least 4 hours in the refrigerator.

2. Make the filling: Peel the potatoes, then mash. You will need 430 g (15 oz). In a bowl, combine the mash with the mint, Parmesan and egg yolk. Season with plenty of white pepper and salt. Mix well, then leave to rest for an hour to allow the flavours to come together.

3. Make the ravioli: Roll out the dough with the help of a pasta machine, making it as thin as possible; you need to be able to almost see through it.

4. Once rolled out, cut the dough into long strips about 6 cm (2½ in) wide. Divide the filling mixture into small balls of about 8 g (1/3 oz) each. Take the first strip and begin placing the filling balls along its length, spacing them about 1 cm (1/2 in) apart. Fold the pasta over lengthways to encase the balls of filling, and pinch the space between each one with your fingers to seal.

5. Using a pasta cutter, trim the bottom edge, then divide the individual ravioli by cutting where you pinched.

6. Repeat with the remaining pasta and filling until you run out of ingredients (make sure you have 8 ravioli per person). Place the finished ravioli on a tray, well spaced out, and cover with a clean tea towel.

7. Cook and assemble: Heat the buerre blanc over a low heat for 2 minutes, stirring with a whisk so it does not separate and retains some volume.

8. Cook the ravioli in a pan of boiling salted water for about 4 minutes; taste to check they are cooked. Drain and tip into a large lukewarm bowl. Add half of the beurre blanc and move the bowl in a circular motion to evenly coat the ravioli in the glossy sauce.

9. Divide between six flat bowls and serve topped with a little more beurre blanc to taste.

CITRUS RISOTTO

<u>Serves 6</u>

I have already spoken extensively about my love for citrus fruits; I use them abundantly and proudly, from entrée to dessert. They work particularly well in risotto, with the natural sweetness and starchiness of Carnaroli rice playing well with the fresh acidity of the citrus. In this risotto, we have played with different expressions of citrus fruits: salted, syrupy, fresh, infused and smoked, layering them in a way that tries to do justice to the extreme complexity of this fantastic ingredient. If you prefer, a simple Vegetable Broth (241) can be used in place of the lemon broth below.

<u>Ingredients</u>

30 g (2¼ oz) olive oil
320 g (10¾ oz/1½ cups) Carnaroli rice
100 g (3½ oz/scant ½ cup) dry white wine
100 g (3½ oz) Beurre Blanc (page 232)
70 g (2¼ oz) freshly grated Parmigiano Reggiano
35 g (1¼ oz) Preserved Lemons (page 242),
    finely chopped
60 g (2 oz) Candied Citrus Paste (page 234)
zest of 1 bergamot

For the lemon broth
3 litres (104 fl oz/12 cups) water
peel of 6 lemons (removed with a peeler)
10 lemon leaves
4 bay leaves
30 g (1 oz) salt

Method

1. Make the broth: Pour the measured water into a large saucepan over a low heat. When it reaches 65°C (149°F), add the lemon peel, lemon leaves and bay leaves. Cover with a lid and take off the heat. Leave to infuse for 2 hours.

2. Strain, add the salt, and return the pan to the heat, bringing the broth to a gentle simmer.

3. Make the risotto: Heat the oil in a large saucepan over a medium heat. Add the rice and toast for about 4 minutes. Deglaze with the wine, then allow the alcohol to evaporate for 1 minute. Now add a ladleful of the citrus broth; it should just barely cover the rice. Cook, stirring often, and making sure the rice always has a few bubbles; it should not be boiling, but neither should the heat be too low. Whenever the broth starts to dry up, add another ladleful. The cooking time will vary depending on the quality of the rice; it can range from 13 to 18 minutes. The important thing is to taste it often so that you can adjust accordingly.

4. When the rice is ready, take the pan off the heat. Add the bergamot zest, beurre blanc (it's best if this is cold from the fridge), Parmigiano and preserved lemon. Cover and leave to sit for 2 minutes, then stir vigorously. It should have a creamy, well-emulsified consistency. You can add a little more broth if it has dried out.

5. Assemble: Divide the risotto between six warm plates, tapping each one lightly on the work surface to spread the rice. Garnish with the candied citrus paste, using a squeezing bottle; its sweetness will contrast with the acidity. Serve immediately.

SLOW-ROASTED PORK SHOULDER, 5 SPICES, GRAPE MOLASSES

Serves 8–10

Approaching the festive season, we loved the idea of having a meat course that felt very grand, to be made only on special occasions, devoting a lot of time and care to its preparation. We like to bring this pork shoulder to the table whole, surrounded by side dishes, preserves and sauces.

This is a cut that is not particularly prized, but lends itself particularly well to this kind of slow and patient cooking. To push it further into the festive mood, we enrich it with plenty of 5-spice mix (that magic combination of cinnamon, fennel, Szechuan pepper, cloves, star anise) and glaze it on the barbecue with vincotto (reduced grape juice), a classic Apulian ingredient that is used extensively in the preparation of traditional sweets at Christmas time.

I have to thank our friend and talented chef Merlin Johnson who, during a collaborative evening in 2019, cooked us an incredible piece of pork, juggling barbecue and oven, giving us an amazing lesson in technique and how to make a great dish from a humble ingredient.

Ingredients

3 kg (6 lb 6 oz) pork shoulder, deboned
6 litres (1.3 gallons) Meat Brine (page 241, substituting seasonings with the spice mix shown here)
1 head of garlic
pickles and preserves of your choice, to serve

For the 5-spice mix
12 whole star anise
6 g (¼ oz) cloves
2 cinnamon sticks
25 g (1 oz) fennel seeds
10 g (½ oz) Szechuan peppercorns

To glaze
300 g (10½ oz) vincotto
20 g (¾ oz) 5-spice mix

Method

1. Make the 5-spice mix: Toast the whole spices in a frying pan for 3 minutes over a medium heat, until fragrant. Blend half of them to a smooth powder and leave the rest whole.

2. Coarsely pound the whole spices in a mortar and use them to flavour the brine for the meat.

3. For the brine: bring the liquid to the boil, then add the pounded spices with the garlic cut in half horizontally, remove from the heat then leave to infuse until completely cooled.

4. Place the pork shoulder in a sufficiently large container and cover with the cold marinade. Make sure the meat is completely submerged, help yourself by placing weights on top if necessary. Place in the fridge to marinate for 12 hours.

5. Drain from the marinade, dry well and, if possible, leave to dry in the fridge on a wire rack, uncovered for a few hours or overnight.

6. The following day, preheat the oven to 90°C (195°F) then place the meat in a roasting tin and cook for 2–2½ hours, until it reaches 65°C (150°F) at the core, checking with a probe thermometer.

7. Light your barbecue and bring the temperature to around 110°C (230°F), using a nicely perfumed wood to get a nice smoky flavour.

8. Brush the shoulder with a third of the vincotto and dust with the ground 5-spice mix to make an even coating. Place the pork shoulder on a baking tray and cook on the barbecue over indirect heat for 1 hour and 30 minutes, repeating the glazing process every 30 minutes until you have a shiny, delicious crust.

9. Allow to rest at room temperature for 2 hours, covering with foil to prevent it from cooling too much.

10. Slice the pork finely and serve with seasonal side dishes, pickles and preserves. The result is usually so juicy that it does not need sauces, especially if accompanied by other elements that balance it out.

MOROSETA

MACKEREL, RAISIN AND CAPER SAUCE, BITTER GREENS

Serves 6

Towards the end of winter, between February and March, we begin to receive excellent mackerel from the Adriatic Sea; the fish are not very large, but they're really tasty and firm. I think mackerel is fantastic; its strong and intense flavour means it can stand up to the boldest combinations and the liveliest cooking, giving you great freedom of expression in the kitchen.

Here, we have paired it with similarly bold flavours for a play on contrasts and edginess, with bitter chicory mellowed by an extraordinary dressing of capers and raisins submerged in brown butter (this was taught to me by Alice during one of our workshops, and has not left our kitchen since that day), as well as our classic broad bean and miso hummus. It is a complex yet sincere dish, extremely Apulian, but also quintessentially ours.

Ingredients

3 medium-sized mackerel
40 g (1½ oz) Wine and Soy Glaze (page 237)
120 g (4¼ oz) Broad Bean Hummus (page 233)
salt

For the raisin and caper sauce
100 g (3½ oz) capers
100 g (3½ oz) raisins
220 g (7¾ oz) Brown Butter (page 233)
6 anchovies
2 garlic cloves, finely sliced
25 g (1 oz/scant 2 tablespoons) apple cider vinegar

For the bitter greens
150 g (5 oz) tender young chicory
35 g (1¼ oz) Garlic Citronette (page 234)

Method

1. Prepare the mackerel: Fillet the mackerel with a sharp knife and remove the spines. Pat the fish dry with paper towels, season with salt and leave to rest for 20 minutes. Meanwhile, fire up the barbecue.

2. Make the sauce: In two separate bowls, soak the capers and raisins in cold water for 20 minutes.

3. Heat the brown butter in a saucepan over a low heat for a few minutes, then add the sliced garlic and anchovies. Reduce the heat to very low and cook for 10 minutes until the mixture is fragrant and the anchovies have completely melted.

4. Drain and squeeze the capers and raisins, then add them to the butter, together with the apple cider vinegar. Take the pan off the heat and leave to rest for 30 minutes.

5. Prepare the bitter greens: Rinse the chicory in cold water. Spin dry, then lay out the leaves on a tray lined with a dry tea towel. Select the nicest, smallest leaves; you will need five per person.

6. Place your chosen leaves in a bowl and add the garlic citronette. Leave to rest for 5 minutes. As chicory is quite sturdy, there is no risk of the leaves becoming too soft. If you're worried they are particularly tender, do this just before you are serving instead.

7. Cook the mackerel and serve: Grill the mackerel fillets on the barbecue, skin-side down, taking care not to position them too close to the coals, as the skin tends to burn quickly. During the final 2 minutes, brush the mackerel with the glaze so that it caramelises evenly.

8. Take out six plates and divide the broad bean hummus between them, placing an even dollop on each one and flattening it with the back of a spoon, creating a hollow. Spoon some of the raisin and caper sauce into this hollow.

9. Add the mackerel fillets to the plates, positioning them sideways so that they partially rest on the hummus. Garnish with the chicory leaves and serve.

CREMA GELATO

Makes 1 kg (2 lb 2 oz)

The base is quite simply the best *crema gelato* I have ever managed to make. Lots of yolks, the right amount of sugar, really good milk and a pinch of salt. The aroma is citrusy (strangely enough), with notes of grapefruit, lemons, bergamot and a final astringent hint of black tea, a bouquet that nicely balances the roundness of this custard base, making it very delicious but also not overly sweet, especially when served at the end of a meal.

Ingredients

600 g (1 lb 3 oz/generous 2 cups) whole milk
peel of 1 lemon
½ peel of grapefruit
½ peel of bergamot
5 g (¼ oz) Earl Grey tea
100 g (4 oz/⅓ cup) double (heavy) cream
8 egg yolks
180 g (6½ oz) caster (superfine) sugar
2 g (⅛ oz) white carob powder
pinch of salt, plus more to serve

Method

1. Make the gelato: In a saucepan over a low heat, heat the milk to 70°C (158°F). Take off the heat, then add the citrus peels and black tea. Stir well, then leave to infuse for 10–12 minutes.

2. Strain through a sieve lined with a piece of muslin (cheesecloth). Weigh the milk, checking that you have 500 g (1 lb 2 oz). Top up the milk if necessary, then pour it into a medium saucepan and add the cream. Gently warm through over a low heat.

3. Meanwhile, in a small bowl, mix the egg yolks with the sugar, carob powder and salt. Slowly pour this mixture into the hot milk and cream and mix well with a whisk. Continue to cook over a low heat, stirring continuously, until the mixture reaches 82°C (180°F).

4. Take the pan off the heat and blend for a few seconds, then pour into a container with a lid. Cool quickly with a blast chiller or ice bath.

5. Once completely cold, place in the refrigerator and leave for 12 hours.

6. Churn and freeze: The following day, quickly blend the mixture again for a few seconds, then add it to your gelato machine and churn according to the manufacturer's instructions.

7. Leave to set for 2 hours in the freezer, and serve with a pinch of salt.

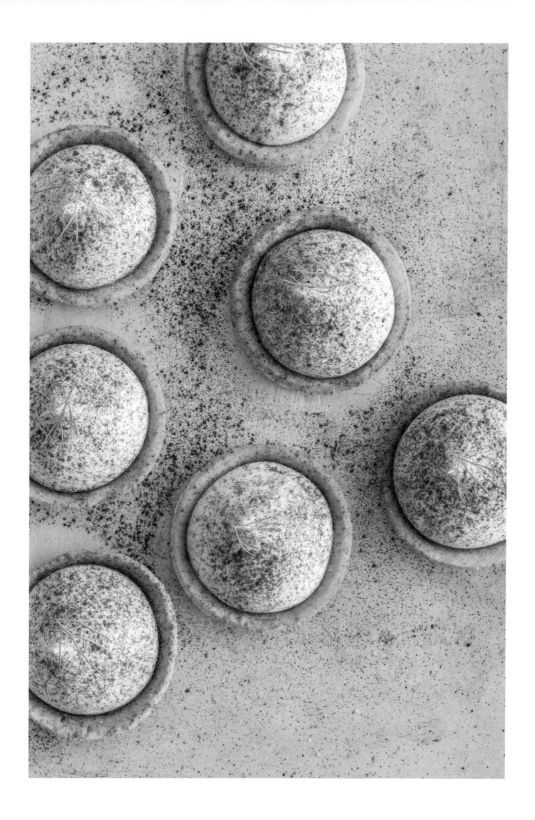

MOROSETA

LEMON CURD, BLACK OLIVE AND CARAMEL TARTLETS, LIQUORICE

Makes 18

I don't remember exactly how I arrived at this combination of flavours, but I remember very well how I felt the first time I ate one of the prototypes. That combination of sweet, savoury and tangy was something really different from what we had been doing up to that point, and I knew with certainty that these little tarts were here to stay.

Served alongside an infusion of bay leaves, sage and honey, these tartlets are one of our favourite ways to end a special meal; they are a token of thanks to our hosts for trusting us, and for allowing us to lead them into our world.

Ingredients

300 g (10½ oz) Pasta Frolla (page 239)
plain (all-purpose) flour, for dusting

For the lemon curd
5 g (¼ oz) gelatine (1 sheet)
zest and juice of 4 lemons (you will need 130 g
    (4½ oz/½ cup) juice)
130 g (4½ oz) egg yolks
125 g (4 oz/generous ½ cup) sugar
210 g (7½ oz) butter, cubed

For the black olive caramel
180 g (6½ oz/generous ¾ cups) sugar
200 g (7 oz) pitted black olives, very finely chopped
15 g (½ oz/1¼ tablespoons) extra virgin olive oil

To finish
liquorice powder, for dusting
salt
fennel

Method

1. **Make the pastry cases:** Set out 18 tartlet moulds (4 cm/1 ½ in diameter, 1.5 cm (5/8 in) deep).

2. Roll out the shortcrust pastry with a rolling pin until very thin (about 3 mm/1/18 in), trying to use as little flour as possible.

3. Chill for 15 minutes, then use a 5 cm (2 in) circular cutter and cut out 18 circles. Prick each one with a fork, then press each one evenly into a tartlet mould, taking care not to deform the dough. Chill in the refrigerator for 1 hour.

4. Preheat the oven to 160°C fan (320°F/gas 4) and bake the tartlet cases for 12 minutes until golden and crispy. Cool on a cooling rack, then place in an airtight container until needed.

5. **Make the lemon curd:** Put the gelatine in a bowl of iced water to soak for a couple of minutes.

6. Meanwhile, pour the lemon juice into a saucepan and bring to a gentle boil over a medium heat.

7. In a bowl, whisk together the egg yolks, lemon zest and sugar. Pour in the hot lemon juice, stirring constantly with the whisk so as not to create lumps or curdle the eggs.

8. Pour the mixture back into the saucepan and place over a low heat. Cook, stirring constantly, until it reaches 82°C (180°F).

9. Take the pan off the heat. Drain and squeeze the gelatine to remove any excess liquid, then add it to the lemon mixture and mix well.

10. Transfer to a bowl and add the cubed butter. Blend with an immersion blender for 2 minutes until completely emulsified, then cover with cling film (plastic wrap), ensuring it makes direct contact with the surface of the curd to prevent a skin from forming. Place in the refrigerator and leave to chill for at least 6 hours.

→ Continued on Following Page

11.   Once cold and set, transfer into a piping bag with a 1 cm (¾ in) nozzle.

12.   Make the caramel: Place the sugar in a heavy-based saucepan and moisten the sides with a few drops of water. Heat over a low–medium heat for 5 minutes to make a caramel. To facilitate melting, you can move the pan in circular motions, but never touch the caramel with a spoon. When it is a dark blonde caramel colour, remove the pan from the heat and add the chopped black olives, olive oil and a pinch of salt. Transfer into a container and leave to stand at room temperature.

13.   Assemble: The tartlets can be assembled about half an hour before serving. If they are made too far in advance, the shortcrust pastry may become soggy and break (see Chef's Notes).

14.   Put 5 g (¼ oz) of the olive caramel in each pastry shell, flattening with a small offset spatula.

15.   On top of the caramel, add 18 g (¾ oz) of lemon curd using the piping bag, giving it a round and regular shape.

16.   Dust with a little liquorice powder and, just before serving, add a pinch of salt and some fresh fennel.

Chef's Notes

Protecting the cases: If you wish, you can opt to waterproof the pastry cases by brushing them with a little melted cocoa butter, which will create a protective layer.

MOROSETA

PICKLED FENNEL, ROSEMARY, ORANGE, AND SUN-DRIED TOMATOES

Makes 3 litre jar

Our variety of pickles is always changing, with varying brine proportions, ingredients and flavourings, but this fennel recipe has now become a classic. The anise-like sweetness of the fennel holds its own unexpectedly well against the liveliness of rosemary, orange, dried tomatoes and garlic, creating a truly unique pickle, elegant but with great character. I remember a customer once told me that she had come back to dinner just to taste that fennel again, as she had been so impressed by its innocent, slightly faded appearance and totally unexpected flavour.

Ingredients

6 medium fennel bulbs
2 oranges
150 g (5 oz) sun-dried tomatoes
6 sprigs rosemary
1 garlic bulb, separated into cloves

For the pickling liquid
900 ml (30½ fl oz/ generous 3½ cups) water
540 ml (18¼ fl oz/generous 2 cups) white wine vinegar
320 g (10¾ oz/1⅓ cups) sugar

Method

1. Prepare the ingredients: Wash the fennel bulbs and cut them into wedges, dividing each into 4–6 even-sized wedges, depending on size. Peel the orange peel with a peeler, taking care to remove as little of the white pith as possible. You can peel the garlic cloves if you want a more intense fragrance; I prefer to leave the skins on. Cut the rosemary into sprigs of about 10 cm (4 in).

2. Alternate the ingredients in a sterilised jar, trying to fill all the spaces well without leaving too many gaps.

3. Prepare the pickling liquid and seal: In a large saucepan over a medium heat, combine the ingredients for the pickling liquid and heat until the sugar has dissolved. Carefully pour this liquid into the vegetable jar and seal tightly.

4. Place the sealed jar in a saucepan of cold water, making sure the water reaches past the lid. Bring to the boil, then simmer for 15 minutes. Take off the heat allow to cool completely in the pan.

5. Leave to pickle for at least 3 weeks before consuming.

MOROSETA

GRAPEFRUIT MARMALADE

Makes 3 x 250 g (10 oz) jars

Of the whole wonderful world of jams, marmalades are at the very top, in my humble opinion. Their goodness is directly proportional to the immense amount of work you have to do to achieve the final result. I researched various recipes and in the end – after consulting with my Aunt Irene, the greatest expert on the subject – I found a medium–fast method that does not involve soaking for days or several consecutive boils. There is a bit more waste compared to the classic recipe, but there is the undeniable satisfaction of being able to make a real marmalade in just a few steps, only observing the basic resting times.

Ingredients

6 pink grapefruits (about 1.7 kg/3 lb 13 oz)
caster (superfine) sugar (see below)

Method

1. Prepare the grapefruits: Wash the grapefruits well, then carefully peel them with a peeler, taking care to remove as little of the white pith as possible. Finely slice the strips of zest; I like them particularly thin, about 2 mm (1/16 in), but the thickness depends on your personal taste.

2. Cut the tops and bottoms off the peeled grapefruits, so that they have a flat surface on which to rest on the cutting board. Working from top to bottom, cut away all the white parts. Cube the resulting pulp, removing any seeds and discarding the fibrous parts.

3. Weigh the obtained pulp and zest, and add 40 per cent of their weight in sugar. (My pulp and zest came to 1 kg (2 lb 4 oz), so I added 400 g (14 oz/1¾ cups) of sugar.) Mix well, then place in a container and leave to macerate for 3–12 hours.

4. Boil the marmalade: After the macerating time has elapsed, transfer the mixture to a heavy-based saucepan. Place over a medium heat and, stirring frequently, bring to the boil. Boil for 4 minutes, then turn off the heat. The marmalade will still have a somewhat sluggish consistency, but the zest will be starting to have a nice shiny appearance. Leave to cool to room temperature, then cover and leave overnight.

5. Finish and seal: The next day, cook the marmalade once more until the desired consistency is achieved. In my case, it took about 30 minutes of gentle simmering. Once you're happy with the consistency, pour the marmalade into sterilised jars, taking care not to leave any air bubbles. Close each jar tightly with a lid.

6. Place the sealed jars in a saucepan of cold water, making sure the water reaches past the lids. Bring to the boil, then simmer for 30 minutes. Take off the heat allow to cool completely in the pan before storing in the pantry, labelled.

Chef's Notes

Consistency: As the marmalade cools, the consistency becomes thicker, especially in the case of citrus fruits that are rich in natural pectin. If it becomes too thick after cooling, you can add a little water and heat it briefly to soften and loosen.

CITRUS GIN

Makes a 3 litre (104 fl oz/12 cup) jar

When the citrus grove decides it's time, it's time, and we find ourselves with *a lot* of fruit to process. This gin was born out of the need for a super-quick preparation that we could make and then leave to steep during the winter break. We use it mainly to give a touch of spirit to herbal teas serve at the end of meals, which always have a small secret alcoholic component. If you have tasted them and wondered what makes them so special and deliciously drinkable, now you know.

Ingredients

1.3 kg (2 lb 4 oz) mixed citrus fruits
1.5 litres (51 fl oz/6 cups) gin
flavourings of your choice (bay leaves, fennel, artemisia, rue, cardamom pods, juniper berries, peppercorns)

Method

1. Prepare the citrus fruit: Sterilise a 3-litre jar.

2. Wash the citrus fruit well. If the peel has some stubborn dirt on it, you can use a small brush to gently scrape it away. Cut the fruit into slices or wedges according to its shape; the smaller the pieces, the more intense the infusion will be. If you leave the citrus fruits whole, the infusion will be slower and gentler.

3. If you decide to use dried spices, toast them briefly in a pan over a medium heat until they are fragrant.

4. Infuse the gin and seal: Alternate the citrus fruits, spices and herbs in the sterilised jar. Pour in the gin, filling the jar up to 1 cm (¾ in) from the rim, making sure that all the ingredients are completely submerged.

5. Seal the jar and allow to stand for at least 6 weeks before straining and using.

05   BASICS

Often when I am asked how I would describe my cooking, I flee from overly poetic and wordy descriptions and take refuge in the honest and simple expression 'great ingredients well-seasoned'. Here you will find our must-have preparations, those that are always in heavy rotation, concentrates of acidity, freshness, crunchiness, sweetness, spicy and umami. Designed to enhance, support and deepen the potential of each ingredient.

DIPS, GLAZES
& SAUCES

ALMOND EMULSION

<u>Makes 500 g (1 lb 2 oz)</u>

The inspiration for this sauce is ajo blanco, a traditional Spanish soup made with stale bread, almonds and copious amounts of garlic. We were intrigued by its enveloping and pungent flavour, but were looking for something with a thicker consistency: spoonable, but not soupy. It works with practically everything and can also be used as an excellent dip for fresh vegetables.

150 g (5 oz/1½ cups) almond flour
15 g (½ oz/1¼ tablespoons) toasted sesame oil
35 g (1¼ oz/2½ tablespoons) extra virgin olive oil
35 g (1¼ oz) white miso
½ garlic clove, grated
5 g (¼ oz/1 teaspoons) salt
200 g (7 oz/scant 1 cup) unsweetened almond milk
20 g (¾ oz/4 teaspoons) rice vinegar

Mix together all the ingredients in a saucepan. Place over a medium heat and bring to the boil, stirring constantly with a whisk until thick. Pour on to a baking tray and spread out, then cover with cling film (plastic wrap) and allow to cool completely to form a thick and fairly dry paste.

About 30 minutes before using, transfer the paste to a blender and emulsify for 30 seconds. If it is still too thick, add a little more almond milk, up to about 80 g (3 oz/5 tablespoons). Blend again, adjusting the flavour and acidity with more rice vinegar if necessary.

ALMOND MAYO

<u>Makes 750 g (1 lb 6 oz)</u>

Yes, that's right, another almond-based sauce. In this case, it is like mayonnaise – enveloping and rich – but because it contains no eggs, it keeps very well for a few days and can be used in case of dietary restrictions.

400 g (14 oz) white almond butter
40 g (1½ oz) white miso
35 g (1¼ oz/2½ tablespoons) toasted sesame oil
30 g (1 oz/2¼ tablespoons) olive oil
35 g (1¼ oz) nutritional yeast
30 g (1 oz/1½ tablespoons) honey
5 g (¼ oz/1 teaspoon) salt
50 g (2 oz/3 tablespoons) rice vinegar
100 g (3½ oz/scant ½ cup) water

Add all the ingredients except the water to a blender. Add half the water and blend at high speed until well combined, adding more water as required (you may not need it all). This will keep in the fridge for 2–3 days.

<u>Chef's Notes:</u>

Variations: This is a fairly neutral base, so it lends itself very well to being flavoured in different ways. *Try adding:*

— grated bottarga: about 40 g/1½ oz for every 500 g
 (1 lb 2 oz) of mayo
— finely chopped salted lemons,
— chopped pickles, harissa or gochujang
— garlic confit paste
— different nuts and seed butters, such as hazelnut,
 peanut, pumpkin seed or sunflower seed butter

BEURRE BLANC

<u>Makes 275 g (9¾ oz)</u>

How can you not love this classic French sauce, which combines the silkiness of butter with the acidity of wine and lemon? I find it particularly effective with risottos, slow-roasted sweet vegetables, fish and seafood.

2 shallots, finely sliced
250 g (9 oz/1 cup) white wine
115 g (4 oz/scant ½ cup) lemon juice
260 g (9¼ oz) butter, cubed
salt

Put the shallots into a small saucepan with a pinch of salt and cook, without fat, for 5 minutes over a low heat. Add the wine and lemon juice and increase the heat to medium. Simmer until the liquid is almost completely reduced, then take off the heat and add the butter. Stir to gently melt the butter in the residual heat. Strain through a sieve to remove the shallots.

Chef's Notes:

Additions: Add extra flavours for variations on this classic beurre blanc sauce. Some favourites include:

— saffron: rehydrate 1 g (1⁄16 oz) of saffron strands in
  a little water and add to the basic sauce
— chopped capers and lemon zest
— freshly chopped herbs such as tarragon and marjoram
— chopped spring onions (scallions)
— chopped anchovies and confit garlic
— grated bottarga

BROAD BEAN HUMMUS

Makes 1 kg (2 lb 4 oz)

I think all our guests are familiar with this recipe. It is a variation on the iconic Apulian dish of dried broad bean purée, which is served year-round with seasonal vegetables, especially leafy greens such as bitter chicory, chard and puntarelle. We have made it into more of a hummus, adjusting the consistency and seasoning. We often serve it with bread and garden vegetables at the start of the tasting menu.

300 g (10½ oz) dried fava beans
2 onions, finely sliced
about 1.5 litres (51 fl oz/6 cups) warm Vegetable
  Broth (page 243)
50 g (2 oz/3¾ tablespoons) olive oil, plus extra for frying
35 g (1¼ oz/2 ½ tablespoons) Garlic Oil (page 244)
6 g (¼ oz/1 teaspoon) salt
25 g (1 oz/scant 2 tablespoons) apple cider vinegar

Soak the broad beans in a bowl of cold water for about 4 hours, then drain. Heat a drizzle of oil in a frying pan over a low heat. Add the onions and cook for 10–15 minutes until translucent. Add the drained broad beans and mix well, then cook for a few minutes to allow them to take on the onion flavour. Pour over the warm broth and simmer gently, for about 1½ hours until the beans are soft, adding a little more broth if necessary.

When ready, transfer to a blender and blend while still warm, adding the oils, salt and vinegar and making sure it is all fully emulsified and smooth. Once cold, the hummus will tend to thicken up and become firmer. It is advisable to always blend it for a few seconds before serving to get the perfect consistency.

Chef's Notes:

Consistency: It's not easy to get the perfect consistency on the first attempt. It depends on the type of broad beans used, and on how much liquid they absorb during cooking. If the consistency is too thick once blended, you can easily adjust it by adding some water, adding a little at a time. If, on the other hand, it is too liquid, it can be thickened with a little almond flour, which will absorb the extra moisture without radically changing the flavour.

BROWN BUTTER

Makes 400 g (14 oz)

This is perhaps one of my favourite ingredients; just smelling it puts me in a good mood. We mostly use it in small amounts, often as one of the last touches before serving. I still remember the first time I ate some grilled savoy cabbage leaves, seasoned with garlic brown butter, lemon and salt – unbeatable!

500 g (1 lb 2 oz) butter

Melt the butter in a medium saucepan over a low–medium heat. As you continue to cook the butter, it will start to bubble; this means it is losing its water component (about 20 per cent). Next, the Maillard reaction will start, in which the proteins caramelise and the butter takes on a more intense colour. This is the most delicate phase; one must be careful not to exceed 130°C (266°F), the temperature at which the butter burns. Strain through a sieve, then keep in an airtight container in the refrigerator until needed. It will keep for up to 3 weeks.

Chef's Notes:

Infusions: Brown butter lends itself to being flavoured with various spices and flavourings. I prefer to add them afterwards rather than during the caramelisation process; a slow infusion at a low temperature avoids distorting the flavours. *Try adding:*

— garlic: crushed and infused over very low heat
— sage, thyme or oregano
— camomile: preferably dried flowers rather than powder
— vanilla: scrape the seeds from pod and infuse off heat
— warm spice mix (page 245) or smoked paprika

CITRONETTE

Makes 250 g (8¾ oz)

When we serve vegetables from the garden, very fresh and picked just before serving, sometimes the only thing they need is a few drops of citronette to make them just a little brighter. It lets their natural flavours shine through.

75 g (2½ oz/5 tablespoons) lemon juice
15 g (½ oz/¾ tablespoon) mild honey
4 g (1/4 oz/1 teaspoon) salt
100 g (3½ oz) scant ½ cup olive oil
50 g (2 oz/3¾ tablespoons) grapeseed oil

In a bowl, mix together the honey, lemon juice and salt, stirring with a whisk. Then add the oils and continue to whisk until completely emulsified. Transfer into a bottle and store in the refrigerator. The citronette tends to separate during storage; simply shake the bottle before use to emulsify again.

Chef's Notes:

Garlic citronette: To make a garlic citronette, follow the recipe as above but use 50 g (2 oz/3¾ tablespoons) each of olive oil, grapeseed oil and Garlic Oil (see page 244).

CANDIED CITRUS PASTE

Makes 300 g (7 oz)

This incredible citrus concentrate adds depth and freshness to dishes. The caramel base gives structure to the sauce, but leaves room for the natural acidity of these extraordinary fruits to shine.

110 g (3¾ oz/½ cup) cane sugar
1 litre (34 fl oz/4 cups) clementine juice, filtered
500 g (1 lb 2 oz/2 cups) orange juice, filtered
330 g (11 oz/11/3 cups) lemon juice, filtered
460 g (1 lb ½ oz/generous 1¾ cups) dry white wine
40 g (1½ oz/2¾ tablespoons) soy sauce
150 g (5 oz) orange zest strips
100 g (3½ oz) lemon zest strips
4 g (¼ oz) bay leaves

In a medium saucepan make a blond caramel with sugar. Add the juices and gently stir – the caramel may bubble up at this point, so be careful. Stir in the wine and soy sauce, then add the citrus zest and bay leaves. Reduce the heat to low and cook for 1 hour until shiny and syrupy. Strain the mixture through a sieve into a jar (see Chef's Notes), then store in the refrigerator until needed. It will keep for two weeks.

Chef's Notes:

Candied citrus: Once strained, you will find a nice amount of translucent candied citrus zest in the sieve. Don't throw this away; it can be blended to make a delicious candied citrus paste.

GARLIC EMULSION

Makes 500 g (1 lb 2 oz)

Between us, we call this 'bagna cauda', even though it is only inspired by the traditional Piedmontese sauce. We were looking for a stable and creamy garlic emulsion, but one that was not too aggressive or overpowering. As much as we love garlic, it is not always easy to include it in recipes without it masking everything else on the menu. After several attempts, we came up with this fantastic sauce, which first involves several blanches to remove the more pungent component of garlic, and then a long and gentle simmering in milk and butter.

190 g (6½ oz) garlic cloves, peeled
140 g (4¾ oz) butter
600 g (1 lb 5 oz/2½ cups) milk
67 g (2¼ oz) white miso
6 g (¼ oz/1 teaspoon) salt
18 g (¾ oz/generous 1 tablespoon) rice vinegar

Place the garlic cloves in a saucepan and cover with cold water. Bring to the boil over a medium heat. Once boiling, drain, then repeat the procedure another 5 times, using fresh water each time. Set aside.

Melt the butter in a medium-sized saucepan over a low heat. Add the blanched garlic cloves and cook for 1 minute until golden. Pour in the milk and cook over low heat for about 30 minutes. Transfer to a blender, along with the miso, salt and vinegar, and blend until smooth.

Chef's Notes:

Anchovy variation: Try adding a few anchovies while browning the garlic, decreasing or removing the miso.

Spicy version: To make a spicy version, use Spicy Vinegar (page 245) instead of rice vinegar, or add a little 'nduja or harissa at the end.

Black garlic emulsion: Adding some black garlic while browning the garlic cloves in butter will give more depth and complexity to the sauce.

MEAT JUS

Makes 250 g (8¾ oz)

Although we don't use a lot of meat, when we do, we use every part of it, trying to reduce waste to zero. The humble meat jus, an iconic preparation in classic cuisine, is something extraordinary when well executed. We like to use it in recipes where there is no other meat element; it can give extraordinary and illusory results.

3 kg (6 lb 12 oz) bones and meat offcuts
60 g (2½ oz) olive oil
600 g (1 lb 5 oz) onions, roughly chopped
1 carrot, roughly chopped
4 celery stalks, roughly chopped
4 litres (135 fl oz) water

Preheat the oven to 210°C fan (410°F/gas 8). Arrange the bones and meat offcuts on a large baking tray. Roast in the oven for 15–20 minutes until it is all a nice caramel colour. Be careful not to let it burn, because then the whole sauce will taste burned.

Meanwhile, heat the olive oil in a large saucepan over a low–medium heat. Add the vegetables and cook for 15 minutes. Add the roasted bones to the pan with the vegetables and pour over the cold water. It should be enough to cover the bones. Bring to the boil, then reduce the heat to low and simmer for 4–6 hours. As it cooks, foam will rise to the surface. This is where impurities are concentrated, so it is important to remove as much of this foam as possible using a slotted spoon.

After the cooking time is up, strain the liquid through a sieve, then return it to a pan over an medium heat and reduce for until thick and glossy. Store in the refrigerator until needed. It will keep for 5 days.

MOROSETA SALAD DRESSING

Makes about 300 g (10 oz)

This is the dressing we always have ready in the fridge, perfect for livening up a sad staff meal or for last-minute salads. Created to satisfy our desire for a bridge between a honey-mustard dressing and a more Asian-inspired one, it works well with both tender and crispier salads.

45 g (1¾ oz/2¼ tablespoons) mild honey
60 g (2 oz/¼ cup) rice vinegar
50 g (2 oz/3 tablespoons) soy sauce
13 g (½ oz) white miso
15 g (½ oz) Dijon mustard
80 g (3 oz/⅓ cup) olive oil
70 g (2¼ oz/generous ¼ cup) grape seed oil

In a bowl, dissolve the honey in the vinegar and soy sauce, stirring with a whisk to combine. Next, add the miso and mustard and mix well. Finish by slowly adding the oils and whisking until fully emulsified. Transfer into a bottle and store in the refrigerator.

PECORINO CHEESE FONDUE

Makes 750 g (1 lb 6 oz)

Few things can beat a good cheese fondue. In the winter months, we often use fondue as a boost sauce, as it has a savoury, umami and silky touch that nicely counterbalances the sweet flavours found in root vegetables, pumpkins and brassicas. We mainly use Pecorino Canestrato, an aged sheep's milk cheese produced in our area.

370 g (13 oz) Pecorino Canestrato, grated
350 g (12 oz/scant 1½ cups) milk
50 g (2 oz/¼ cup) cream

In a medium saucepan over a medium heat, bring the milk and cream to the boil. Tip the grated cheese into another saucepan off the heat, then pour the hot milk and cream over the top. Let it stand for 2 minutes, then stir well with a whisk and place over a low heat to bring it back to 65°C (149°F). Keep it at this temperature for a few minutes (see Chef's Notes).

Transfer to a blender and blend for a few seconds to obtain a smooth and well emulsified sauce. If it looks a little grainy, you can pass it through a sieve.

The sauce should be served lukewarm, as it tends to solidify quickly, so when you're ready to serve, warm it up gently over a low heat or in a bain-marie.

Chef's Notes:

The perfect temperature: In the kitchen, we usually make this using a Thermomix so that we have perfect temperature control, so do use one if you can. If not, use a thermometer, and take care to work over a low heat.

SOY SAUCE AND WINE GLAZE

Makes 250 g (8¾ oz)

I have to be honest, in the kitchen we call this 'fake jus', since this caramelised, savoury and umami glaze is very reminiscent of a meat sauce. It is a perfect way to add a final depth of flavour or to add that delicious gloss before serving. It keeps for weeks in the fridge, so I recommend making a generous amount.

100 g (3½ oz) sugar
550 g (1 lb 4 oz/19 fl oz/2¼ cups) dry white wine
60 g (2 oz/¼ cup) shoyu soy sauce

4 garlic cloves, peeled
20 g (¾ oz) sage leaves
18 g (¾ oz) rosemary sprigs
90 g (3¼ oz) fresh root ginger, sliced

In a heavy-based saucepan over a medium heat, heat the sugar with a few drops of water until it forms a light caramel. Take the pan off the heat, and pour in the remaining ingredients. The liquids may splash a little, so be careful. Return to the heat and simmer for 40 minutes until you have a slightly syrupy consistency. Strain out the herbs and ginger, then pour into a squeezing bottle. It will keep in the fridge for three weeks.

Chef's Notes:

Different aromas: We have opted for flavourings that are very reminiscent of meat-based recipes, precisely to further emphasise that illusion of mock meat jus. However, you can opt for different aromas, resulting in different nuances. Try adding juniper berries, cinnamon, cumin, black pepper or chilli.

Additions: After cooking, you can add some extra characterising elements, such as a few drops of fish sauce, a little chilli paste, such as harissa or gochujang, some mustard seeds, or a dash of honey.

SPICY HONEY

Makes 1.3 kg (2 lb 8 oz)

One year, we produced an incredible amount of chillies in the garden, and we really didn't know what to do with them all. We stumbled upon this honey recipe almost by chance. We simply combined the ingredients and let it sit in the pantry for a few months to see what would happen. The result is very useful for adding a touch of spiciness to marinades and dressings, and suitable in both sweet and savoury dishes.

50 g (2 oz) fresh chillies (medium heat),
*   halved lengthways*
16 g (½ oz) mustard seeds
5 thyme sprigs
1.2 kg (2 lb 11 oz) honey
100 g (3½ oz/scant ½ cup) water

Place the chillies, mustard seeds and thyme in a sterilised jar and set aside. Combine the honey and water in a medium-sized saucepan over a low-medium heat, and heat for until the mixture is liquid and hot (it should not boil). Pour the honey mixture into the jar, making sure all the ingredients are covered. Close tightly and allow to rest for 3 months before using.

TAHINI SAUCE

Makes 300 g (10 oz)

This is a super-versatile sauce that we use very often in many different dishes. Its slightly bitter taste goes well with grilled and roasted vegetables and earthy salads, and it also makes an excellent dip.

150 g (5 oz) tahini
2 g (1/8 oz/½ teaspoon) salt
35 g (1¼ oz) white miso
22 g apple cider vinegar
27 g toasted sesame oil
10 g (½ oz/2 teaspoons) Garlic Oil (page 244)
25 g (1 oz/ 1¼ tablespoons) honey
50 g (2 oz/3 tablespoons) water

Combine all the ingredients in a blender and emulsify until you have a smooth, glossy sauce. If it is too thick, you can adjust with a little water at a time. This will keep in the fridge for two weeks.

BAKING BASICS

ALMOND CRUMBLE

Makes 900 g (2 lb)

When we have to assemble a plated dessert, a bit of crumble never goes amiss, and those buttery, crunchy crumbs are often the most delicious and appreciated part. This is the basic recipe, but it lends itself to endless variations with different flours and flavourings.

240 g (8 ½ oz/scant 1 cup) plain (all-purpose) flour
240 g (8 ½ oz/generous 1 cup) cane sugar
200 g (7 oz) butter, cold
200 g (7 oz/2 cups) almond flour
5 g (¼ oz/1 teaspoon) salt

Place all the ingredients in a bowl and rub together with your fingertips until you obtain large crumbs. Press the mixture together to form a small ball. Wrap this in cling film (plastic wrap) and leave to rest in the fridge for 6 hours.

To bake, preheat the oven to 170°C fan (340°F/has 5) and line a baking tray with baking parchment. Crumble the crumble mixture on to the prepared tray. Be careful not to pile the pieces too close together, or you risk creating one huge crumble cookie. Bake for 15–20 minutes until evenly golden. Leave to cool, then transfer to an airtight container until needed.

SAVOURY CRUMBLE

Makes 800 g (1 lb 7 oz)

We were looking for a savoury and mouth-watering counterpart to our classic sweet crumble.

By assembling a bit of what was on hand, such as stale bread, some leftover chestnut flour from another preparation and a generous handful of Parmesan cheese, this rough dough was born. Perfect for giving texture, umami and a gourmand touch to plant-based preparations.

100 g (3½ oz) stale bread
140 g (5 oz/generous 1 cup) plain (all-purpose) flour
170 g (6 oz) Parmesan cheese, grated
30 g (1 oz) brown sugar
200 g (7 oz) butter, cold
80 g (3 oz/¾ cup) almond flour
100 g (3½ oz/1 cup) chestnut flour
5 g (¼ oz/1 teaspoon) salt
2 g (1/8 oz/½ teaspoon) freshly ground black pepper

Using a food processor, blend the bread to a fine, sandy texture. Tip this into a mixing bowl, and add the remaining ingredients. Rub together with your fingertips until you obtain large crumbs. Press the mixture together to form a small ball. Wrap this in cling film (plastic wrap) and leave to rest in the fridge for 6 hours.

To bake, preheat the oven to 170°C fan (340°F/gas 5) and line a baking tray with baking parchment.

Crumble the crumble mixture on to the prepared tray. Be careful not to pile the pieces too close together, or you risk creating one huge crumble cookie. Bake for 15–20 minutes until evenly golden. Leave to cool, then transfer to an airtight container until needed.

PASTA FROLLA

Makes 600 g (1 lb 5 oz)

This sweet shortcrust pastry is an adaptation of a historical recipe by Pellegrino Artusi, one of the most important chefs in the history of Italian gastronomy.

270 g (9 ½ oz/generous 2 cups) '00' flour
115 g (4 oz/scant 1 cup) icing (confectioner's) sugar
135 g (4¾ oz) butter, at room temperature
4 egg yolks (about 65 g/2¼ oz)
zest of 1 lemon (optional)
5 g (¼ oz/1 teaspoon) salt

In the bowl of a stand mixer, cream the soft butter with the icing sugar, salt and lemon zest (if using). We are not trying to incorporate air, so just work at low speed with the flat beater attachment until the ingredients are well blended.

Add the egg yolks gradually, making sure they are well combined, then sift in half of the flour. Mix, then sift in the rest. The dough will be quite soft; do not be alarmed. From it into a flat dough ball and cover with cling film (plastic wrap). Let it rest in the refrigerator for 6 hours before using as instructed in your recipe.

Chef's Notes:

Freeze: I usually make more pastry than I need, let it rest for the time indicated, then divide it into portions to freeze, so that I always have some ready to use. It is advisable to form it into fairly flat dough balls for freezing, as they will defrost quickly and are easier to roll out.

Flavourings: This base can be flavoured in many different ways, depending on how you want to use it. Add the flavourings at the same time as the icing sugar:

— fennel seeds and lemon zest
— vanilla and freshly ground black pepper
— tonka bean and coffee
— coriander seeds and orange zest
— ground cinnamon and ginger
— ground cardamom and bergamot zest

OLIVE OIL PAN BRIOCHE

Makes 1 loaf

When I asked Luca Lacalamita, genius mastermind, trusted friend and baker behind all things bakery-related at Moroseta, to develop a recipe for fluffy but dairy-free pan brioche, he immediately accepted the challenge. After a few days of experimenting, he sent me this incredible, fluffy bread with a great texture, fragrance and balance.

In all honesty, this is quite difficult to perfect, even though Luca would probably describe it as pretty simple if I 'just follow the instructions'. I have listed the bread starters used by Luca, but please feel free to use what you have to hand rather than creating three.

150 g (3½ oz) water
500 g (1 lb 1 oz) type 1 flour
150 g (3½ oz) bread starter (divided into 50 g strong
    flour starter, 50 g San Francisco style wholemeal
    starter, 50 g rye starter)
150 g (3½ oz) unsweetened almond milk
112 g (3 oz) extra virgin olive oil
20 g (¾ oz) sugar
15 g (½ oz) salt

Prepare an autolysis for 45 minutes with the water and the flour. Add the starter and knead at low speed for 4 minutes. Add one part almond milk with dissolved salt and sugar and knead for a further 7 minutes at medium speed.

Add the remaining water and allow the dough to stick together. Add the olive oil 3 times, always working at medium speed, and knead the dough for a further 7 minutes until completely absorbed.

Stop the dough and let it rest in its bowl for 10 minutes. Place the dough in a plastic box greased with some oil — do 2 cycles of stretch and fold every 30 minutes at room temperature, then leave to rest and ferment at 28ºC (83ºF) for 3 hours.

Break the dough into 340 g (12 oz) balls and place in a loaf tin for a total weight of about 1 kg (2 lb 4 oz) — leave to rise slowly for 12 hours at 15ºC (30ºF).

Preheat the oven to 175ºC (350ºF/gas 5), bake the pan brioche for 45 minutes. Check it is cooked through and immediately unmould as soon as it is ready.

Cool for about 5 hours and serve.

BRINES, BROTHS & PRESERVING

BRINE (FOR MEAT)

Makes enough to marinate 1–3 kg (2 lb 4 oz–6 lb 8 oz) meat

This is the liquid marinade we use to season our meat perfectly, especially lamb and pork. It is very aromatic and intense; you can reduce quantities or replace ingredients, depending on your tastes.

2 litres (70 fl oz/8 cups) water
400 g (14 oz1¾ cups) salt
400 g (14 oz/1¾ cups) sugar
12 g (½ oz) garlic
30 g (1 oz) fresh root ginger, sliced
4 g (¼ oz) bay leaves
20 g (¾ oz) sage leaves
10 g (½ oz) rosemary sprigs
20 g (¾ oz) shoyu soy sauce
zest of 2 lemons

Combine the water, salt and sugar in a medium-sized saucepan and bring to the boil. Take the pan off the heat and add all the remaining ingredients, then cover with a lid and allow to cool completely.

Once cool, immerse the meat in the marinade and leave in the refrigerator for 2–12 hours, depending on the size and thickness of the meat (see below).

Remove from the marinade and cook meat as instructed.

Chef's Notes:

Marinating times: Chicken thighs will need about 2 hours to marinate; a leg of lamb will need about 6 hours; and a pork shoulder about 12 hours.

FISH BROTH

Makes 250 g (8¾ oz)

Just as with meat, if we use fish, every component is used, including the bones. This fumet is delicious and is essential in our kitchen for the preparation of soups and pasta sauces, where it is paired with seafood, legumes and herbs.

3 kg (6 lb 12 oz) fish bones and offcuts
60 g (2½ oz) olive oil
300 g (10½ oz) celery, preferably the white part, chopped
600 g onions, chopped
150 g (5 oz) leek, preferably the white part, chopped
1 fennel bulb, cubed
4 litres (135 fl oz) water

Preheat the oven to 210°C fan (410°F/gas 8).

The most important part is to clean the fish well; remove eyes, gills and any blood residue that would make the sauce bitter. If the fish offcuts are particularly dirty, they can be soaked in cold water to clean them further. Once cleaned, dry well with kitchen paper.

Arrange the bones and scraps on a large baking tray and roast for 10–15 minutes until it is all a nice caramel colour. Be careful not to let it burn, because then the whole sauce will taste burned.

Meanwhile, heat the oil in a large saucepan, over a low–medium heat. Add the vegetables and cook for 10 minutes without browning.

Add the roasted bones to the pan with the vegetables and pour over the cold water; it should be enough to cover the bones. Bring to the boil, then reduce the heat to low and simmer for 2 hours.

After the cooking time is up, strain the liquid through a sieve, then return it to a pan over an medium heat and reduce until thick and glossy. Pour into a container and store in the refrigerator until needed. It will keep for 3 days.

PICKLES

Makes 1.75 kg (3 lb 8 oz)

Pickled vegetables and fruit are the cornerstones of our kitchen. Not only is pickling an incredible way to preserve and use the abundance a season may bring, but it also creates an exciting pantry full of elements that will bring nuance and brightness to any dish.

We use firm, unblemished seasonal fruit and vegetables. I've shared some of my favourite combinations below, but you can choose whatever you want. Be creative!

For the pickling brine
1 litre (40 fl oz/4 cups) water
550 g (1 lb 4 oz/19 fl oz/2¼ cups) white wine vinegar
180 g (6½ oz/generous ¾ cup) sugar
pinch of salt

For pickled beetroots
3 beetroots, peeled, trimmed and sliced into
    2 mm (1/16 in) slices
2 garlic cloves, peeled
4 thyme sprigs

For pickled carrots
4 carrots, peeled, trimmed and sliced
    lengthways or cut into coins
4 cm (1½ in) piece of fresh root ginger, peeled and sliced
½ teaspoon chilli flakes

For pickled cauliflower
1 cauliflower, divided into florets
½ teaspoon freshly grated turmeric
3 bay leaves
1 teaspoon black pepper

For pickled onions
3 Tropea onions, halved and sliced into 5 mm
    (¼ in) slices
1 teaspoon juniper berries, lightly toasted
2 sprigs sage

Combine all the ingredients for the pickling brine in a saucepan and bring to the boil. While you wait, arrange your prepared vegetables and aromatics in a sterilised jar. Pour over the hot brine until the vegetables are completely covered and the jar is full. Seal, then leave to cool.

These pickles will keep in the fridge for up to 2 months. It is advisable to let them marinate for at least a week.

Chef's Notes:

Vinegar: There is no need to use a fancy expensive vinegar, since you are going to add aromatics, water and sugar. I normally use the basic white wine vinegar you find at the supermarket. Rice vinegar also works well because it is neutral.

Substitutions: You can change the proportions of the brine, playing with acidity and sweetness. For example, try making it with three parts water, two parts vinegar and one part sugar, or for a different flavour, one part water, one part vinegar and one part sugar.

Extra brine?: Don't throw away and leftover brine; keep it in a jar for a last-second pickle session!

Short on time?: If you need pickles but do not have a week to spare, you can solve this by cutting the vegetables very finely. This will speed up the pickling process, and they'll be ready to enjoy in just a few hours.

PRESERVED LEMONS

Makes 1 kg (2 lb 2 oz) jar

When lemons are in season and the garden produces plenty, we always make a large batch of these. They are a magical ingredient; just a small amount of finely chopped peel can give flavour and depth to the blandest of dishes, imparting acidity, savouriness and something balsamic and complex created by the fermentation.

1 kg (2 lb 4 oz) lemons, washed
80–100 g (3–3½ oz) salt

Cut a deep cross lengthways into each of the lemons, leaving one of the two ends intact, to create the classic flower cut. Rub the salt into the cuts, working in a bowl so that you don't lose any of the salt that falls out during this process.

Once all the lemons have been salted, pack them into a large jar, making sure they are close together and leaving as little empty space as possible. Add the leftover salt, then put a weight on top of the lemons to encourage them to release their juices. Close the jar and leave at room temperature in a cool place, away from direct light. If the lemons are not covered with liquid in a couple of days, you can add some lemon juice.

The lemons will be ready after about 2 months, depending on the thickness of the peel and the temperature outside.

Chef's Notes:

Other citrus: You can apply the same technique to different citrus fruits, such as oranges, mandarins and kumquats. I recommend avoiding the more bitter citrus fruits, such as bergamots and grapefruits.

VEGETABLE BROTH

Makes 2.5 litres (85 fl oz)

This is the broth we use for a little bit of everything. We put it on the stove first thing as soon as we enter the kitchen. While we start organizing the rest of the work, the broth infuses gently, acquiring a delicate and elegant taste, perfect for many preparations.

We cook it for just over an hour at a relatively low temperature, to keep the flavor clean and the broth crystal clear.

3 litres (104 fl oz/12 cups) water
2 celery stalks, coarsely chopped
3 carrots, coarsely chopped
1 onion, coarsely chopped
30 g (1 oz/2 tablespoons) salt

Combine all the ingredients in a large saucepan over a low heat and cook gently for 1 hour, keeping the temperature at about 80–85°C (175–185°F). This will give you a gently infused, clear broth. Strain and use as desired.

Chef's Notes:

Adding aroma: You can add other ingredients to these basic elements to make your broth more distinctive. Try adding peppercorns, a couple of cloves, some ginger, fresh herbs, citrus peel, seaweed or mushrooms.

VINEGARS, OILS & SPICES

BAY LEAF OIL

Makes 500 g (17 g oz/2 cups)

You will find this bay leaf oil in many recipes in this book; it is a constant presence in our kitchen and is one of my favourite last touches. It lends a balsamic and herbaceous note that goes very well with our type of cooking. We use it so much that last year we planted several new bay laurel bushes, because the old ones were no longer able to meet the required quantities.

36 g (1¼ oz) bay leaves
500 g (1 lb 2 oz/2 cups) grapeseed oil

Bring a saucepan of water to the boil. Add the bay leaves and blanch for 50 seconds, then remove with a slotted spoon and transfer into a bowl of iced water. Drain, then blot the leaves well with paper towel.

Pour the oil into a saucepan over a low heat. Heat to 65°C (149°F) and add the leaves. Keep the temperature constant for an hour.

Transfer to a blender and blend at maximum speed for 1 minute, then strain through a piece of muslin (cheesecloth). Transfer the bay leaf oil into a squeezing bottle and store in the fridge. It will keep for two weeks.

GARLIC OIL

Makes 500 g (17 oz/2 cups)

Since Manu started working with us, garlic has become a distinctive element in the kitchen. However, when working with tasting menus, we must be careful with polarising elements like garlic, chilli or spices. Not being able to grate and chop garlic cloves everywhere as Manu would like, we started using this oil that has the wonderful aroma of garlic, without the pungent, lethal aftertaste.

500 g (1 lb 2 oz/2 cups) grapeseed oil
2 garlic bulbs, cloves peeled

Pour the oil into a saucepan over a low heat. Heat to 80°C (176°F) and add the garlic cloves. Keeping the temperature constant, heat for 1 hour. Strain through a piece of muslin (cheesecloth), keeping the garlic aside (see Chef's Notes). Transfer the oil into a squeezing bottle and store in the fridge. It will keep for two weeks.

Chef's Notes:

Confit: That translucent garlic obtained at the end is nothing but garlic confit, which you can now use in other recipes. It can be stored covered with a little oil.

Add aromatics: This oil lends itself to other flavours. Try adding woody herbs like rosemary, oregano and marjoram, or chilli peppers or lemon zest.

SPICY OIL

Makes 500 g (17 oz/2 cups)

A good spicy oil is an excellent weapon to have in your pantry; a few drops, combined with a little acidity, can elevate even the least interesting of recipes. Over the years, we have made many variations on this theme, using different types of chillies from the garden and exploring different levels of spiciness. This version is similar to an Asian chilli oil: aromatic and complex.

500 g (1 lb 2 oz/2 cups) grapeseed oil
2 fresh chillies (medium heat), halved lengthways

3 garlic cloves, peeled and halved
1 star anise
1 cinnamon stick
5 g (¼ oz) Szechuan peppercorns
10 g (½ oz) smoked chilli flakes
10 g (½ oz) Korean chilli flakes

Pour the oil into a saucepan over a low heat. Heat to 85°C (185°F) and add the fresh chillies, garlic, star anise, cinnamon and Szechuan peppercorns. Keeping the temperature constant, heat for 45 minutes, then add the chilli flakes and continue at the same temperature for another 15 minutes. Strain through a piece of muslin (cheesecloth). Transfer the oil into a squeezing bottle and store in the fridge. It will keep for two weeks.

'NDUJA OIL

Makes 600g (1 lb 3 oz)

Nduja is a typical Calabrian ingredient, a paste made from pork fat and an outrageous amount of dried, lightly smoked chilli peppers. When dissolved in neutral oil, it creates a delicious, complex condiment, somewhat mitigating its proverbial spiciness.

100 g (4 oz) 'nduja
500 g (1 lb 2 oz/2 cups) grapeseed oil

Pour the oil into a saucepan over a low heat. Heat to 80°C (176°F) and add the 'nduja. Keeping the temperature constant, heat for 15 minutes. Blend at high speed for one minute, strain through a piece of muslin (cheesecloth).

Transfer the nduja oil into a squeezing bottle and store in the fridge. It will keep for 2 weeks.

CARPIONE VINEGAR

For a 3 litre (104 fl oz/12 cup) jar

The term 'carpione' refers to a traditional Italian method that involves marinating meat, fish or vegetables in a mixture of vinegar and aromatics, such as sage, garlic and bay leaves. We decided to concentrate these aromatics in a vinegar, and it immediately became a must in our kitchen. It is extremely aromatic and elegant at the same time. We particularly like to use it with sweet roasted vegetables.

400 g (14 oz) celery stalks, chopped into
  10 cm (4 in) pieces
2 garlic bulbs, halved horizontally
20 g (¾ oz) bay leaves
30 g (1 oz) sage leaves
5 g (¼ oz) white peppercorns
2.3 litres (80 fl oz/9¼ cups) white wine vinegar
185 g (6½ oz) honey

Sterilise a 3-litre jar with a hermetic seal, then add the celery, garlic, bay leaves, sage leaves and peppercorns.

In a large bowl or jug, mix the honey with a small amount of vinegar to loosen it. Once loosened, add the rest of the vinegar. (If the honey has crystallised, you can warm this mixture slightly to make it easier to work with). Pour this mixture into the jar and seal. Place the sealed jar in a pan of cold water, making sure the water reaches past the lid. Bring to the boil, then simmer for 30 minutes. Take off the heat and leave to cool in the pan.

Label the jar and allow to stand for 2 months before using. Once opened, strain to remove the aromatics and store the vinegar in the fridge. It will keep for 3 months once opened.

Chef's Notes:

Spray it: It is very practical to keep a small quantity of your flavoured vinegar in a spray bottle. This is perfect for dosing small quantities and enables you to distribute the vinegar evenly over the ingredients, without risking using too much.

SPICY VINEGAR

Makes 1.6 litres (54 fl oz)

Sometimes I think I would like to incorporate more chilli into the food at Moroseta, however, as we only serve a tasting menu, I try not to include anything too spicy without knowing the tastes of our guests. As a

compromise, we started to incorporate components to dishes that could give a touch of heat without excessive spiciness, such as this vinegar, which is perfect for balancing sauces and dressings.

760 g (27 fl oz) cider vinegar
500 g (18 fl oz) water
6 g (¼ oz/1 teaspoon) fish sauce
300 g (10 ½ oz) honey
50 g (1¾ oz) fresh chillies (follow your own
  preference of variety for heat)

Bring the vinegar, water, fish sauce, sugar and honey to a gentle simmer over a medium-high heat. Place the chillies in a sterilized jar, then take the pan from the heat and pour over. Allow to cool, then seal the jar and let infuse for two weeks before using.

WARM SPICES

Makes 100 g (4 oz)

This is a blend we created to pack all our favourite warm spices together. It works effectively in both sweet and savoury recipes. Sometimes it is more practical to have a ready-made and trusted blend, rather than having to open 15 different containers!

25 g (1 oz) coriander seeds
15 g cinnamon sticks
15 g fennel seeds
1 nutmeg
2 g (⅛ oz) cloves
3 g (⅛ oz) juniper berries
15 g (½ oz) ground ginger
10 g (½ oz) ground turmeric
15 g (½ oz) sweet paprika
5 g (¼ oz) black pepper
5 g (¼ oz) allspice

Toast all the whole spices in a dry frying pan over a medium heat for 3 minutes until they are fragrant and the seeds begin to brown slightly.

Transfer to a blender or spice grinder and blend to a fine powder. Add the ground spices and mix well. Keep in an airtight container.

INDEX

A

aguachile, white turnip, nectarine, green tomato 87
almond butter: almond mayo 232
almond flour
    almond crumble 242
    almond emulsion 232
almond emulsion
    artichokes, chestnuts and almond emulsion 199–201
    courgettes, figs, hazelnuts 78
almond milk: kabocha squash soup, 'nduja red prawns 193
almonds
    beet, almond, bottarga 134
    cuttlefish 'tagliatella', almond, miso, wild fennel 98–9
amberjack, citrus, kimchi 139
anchovies
    anchovy brown butter 56–7
    gremolata 28–9
    tomato and anchovy 92
aperitivo 21
apples
    apple, spelt and coriander cake 178
    celeriac and apple soup 144–5
apricots
    apricot compote 126
    apricot sorbet 120–1
artichokes 195
    artichokes, chestnuts and ajo blanco 199–201
    flavour combinations 196
asparagus 33
    flavour combinations 34
    grilled asparagus, gremolata and tahini sauce 28–9
aubergine, black garlic, summer herbs 94
autumn 130–81

B

baking basics 242–3
barbecued oysters, spicy strawberry dressing 46
basil, strawberry and 69
bay leaf oil 245
bee pollen, semolina, fennel and olive oil crackers, whipped
    ricotta, spicy honey, 42–3
beef
    beef tartare, black garlic, daikon, nasturtium 142
    skirt steak, sour plum, pearl onions 111
beetroot
    beet, almond, bottarga 134
    pickled beetroot 240
    strawberry, beetroot and chilli sorbet 71

beurre blanc 232–3
    citrus risotto 210
bitter greens, mackerel, raisin and caper sauce, 215
bombette: pork *bombette*, radicchio, quince 168–9
bottarga
    artichokes and bottarga 196
    beet, almond, bottarga 134
    ricotta and bottarga gnocchi, anchovy brown butter
        and bitter greens 56–7
brassica risotto 153
bread
    fried eggs on toast with kimchi butter 185
    olive oil pan brioche 243
    raviolo 'pane e pomodoro' in tomato broth 100–3
    savoury crumble 242
breakfast 21
brine (for meat) 239
broad (fava) beans
    braised rabbit tortellini, spring broth, wild garlic 50–3
    broad bean dumplings, pepper sauce 104
    broad bean hummus 233
    fava bean, sea urchin, mint risotto 54
broths
    braised rabbit tortellini, spring broth, wild garlic 50–3
    croaker, onion, thyme 165
    kimchi tortellini, celeriac broth, kombu 146–9
    raviolo 'pane e pomodoro' in tomato broth 100–3
    vegetable broth 241
brown butter 233–4
    anchovy brown butter 56–7
    barbecued oysters, spicy strawberry dressing 46
    cumin brown butter 162
    mackerel, raisin and caper sauce, bitter greens 215
    smoked spring onions, chestnut honey and hazelnuts 30–1
buckwheat, cauliflower soup, egg yolk, 203
butter
    anchovy brown butter 56–7
    beurre blanc 232–3
    brown butter 233–4
    chicken liver pâté 136
    cumin brown butter 162
    kimchi butter 185
    mackerel, raisin and caper sauce, bitter greens 215

C

cabbage: red cabbage, orange, lamb jus 162
cakes
    apple, spelt and coriander cake 178
    sbrisolona with polenta, hazelnut, tangerine 177
candied citrus paste: monks beard, pickled garlic, candied citrus 38

capers: mackerel, raisin and caper sauce, bitter greens 215

caramel: lemon curd, black olive and caramel tartlets
with liquorice 219–21

cardoncelli mushrooms, pickled shiitake and 132–3

carpione vinegar 244

carpione vinaigrette 134

carrots

pickled carrots 240

winter giardiniera 187

cauliflower

cauliflower soup, egg yolk, buckwheat 203

pickled carrots 240

winter giardiniera 187

celeriac

celeriac and apple soup 144–5

celeriac confit 144–5

kimchi tortellini, celeriac broth, kombu 146–9

celery: carpione vinegar 244

cheese

artichokes and fresh cheese 196

brassica risotto 153

citrus risotto 210

Delica squash gnocchi, pecorino, Jerusalem artichoke 158–61

flat peach, cucumber, mozzarella 82

Pecorino cheese fondu 236

pumpkin and mature cheese 156

savoury crumble 242

smoked potato plin, saffron beurre blanc 208–9

strawberries and fresh cheese 69

see also mascarpone; ricotta

cherry sorbet 118

chestnut flour: savoury crumble 242

chestnuts: artichokes, chestnuts and ajo blanco 199–201

chicken liver pâté 136

chickpeas: pasta e ceci 206–7

chicory: mackerel, raisin and caper sauce, bitter greens 215

chillies

spicy honey 237

strawberries and chilli 69

strawberry, beetroot and chilli sorbet 71

chips, Jerusalem artichoke 158–61

chocolate: pane e cioccolato 64

cime di rapa (turnip greens): brassica risotto 153

cinnamon, tomato and 92

citronette 234

citrus fruit

amberjack, citrus, kimchi 139

candied citrus paste 234

citrus gin 228

citrus risotto 210

citrus salad 204

see also lemons; oranges, etc

clementine juice: candied citrus paste 234

coconut milk: pasta e ceci 206–7

compote, apricot 126

coriander seeds: apple, spelt and coriander cake 178

courgettes, figs, hazelnuts 78

crackers, semolina, fennel and olive oil 42–3

crema gelato 216

croaker, onion, thyme 165

crumble

almond crumble 242

savoury crumble 242

cucumber: flat peach, cucumber, mozzarella 82

cumin brown butter 162

custard: pane e cioccolato 64

cuttlefish 'tagliatella', almond, miso, wild fennel 98–9

D

daikon: beef tartare, black garlic, daikon, nasturtium 142

Delica squash gnocchi, pecorino, Jerusalem artichoke 158–61

dinner 21–2

dressings

Moroseta salad dressing 235–6

spicy strawberry dressing 46

see also vinaigrettes

drinks

citrus gin 228

smoked quince and five-spice shrub 180

strawberry and lavender shrub 72

dumplings: broad bean dumplings, pepper sauce 104

E

eggs

asparagus and eggs 34

cauliflower soup, egg yolk, buckwheat 203

fried eggs on toast with kimchi butter 185

elderflower vinegar 74

spring garden salad 36

emulsions

almond emulsion 232

garlic emulsion 234–5

F

fennel

cuttlefish 'tagliatella', almond, miso, wild fennel 98–9

pickled fennel, rosemary, orange, and sun-dried
tomatoes 225

winter giardiniera 187

fennel seeds: semolina, fennel and olive oil crackers 42–3

fig leaves
    fig leaf gelato 118, 120–1
    red mullet in fig leaf 112
figs: courgettes, figs, hazelnuts 78
fish
    amberjack, citrus, kimchi 139
    anchovy brown butter 56–7
    croaker, onion, thyme 165
    fish fumet 239
    gremolata 28–9
    mackerel, raisin and caper sauce, bitter greens 215
    red mullet in fig leaf 112
    sea bream, seared lettuce, lardo 59
    tomato and anchovy 92
flowers, edible: spring garden salad 36
fondu, Pecorino cheese 236
fumet, fish 239

G
galette, peach 122–5
garlic
    artichokes and garlic 196
    aubergine, black garlic, summer herbs 94
    beef tartare, black garlic, daikon, nasturtium 142
    carpione vinegar 244
    garlic emulsion 234–5
    garlic oil 245
    monks beard, pickled garlic, candied citrus 38
    rabbit rillettes 190
    slow roasted pork shoulder, 5 spices, grape molasses 213
    tomato risotto, garlic, lemon 106–7
    citrus risotto 210
gazpacho, roasted vegetable 80–1
gelato 117
    crema gelato 216
    fig leaf gelato 118, 120–1
    flavour combinations 118
    potato-skin gelato 170
gin, citrus 228
glaze, soy sauce and wine 236
gnocchi
    Delica squash gnocchi, pecorino, Jerusalem artichoke 158–61
    ricotta and bottarga gnocchi, anchovy brown butter and
        bitter greens 56–7
goat's milk: cauliflower soup, egg yolk, buckwheat 203
grape molasses, slow roasted pork shoulder, 5 spices, 213
grapefruit
    citrus salad 204
    grapefruit marmalade 227
gremolata: grilled asparagus, gremolata and tahini

sauce 28–9
guanciale: octopus, percoca, guanciale kushiyaki 108

H
hazelnuts
    courgettes, figs, hazelnuts 78
    sbrisolona with polenta, hazelnut, tangerine 177
    smoked spring onions, chestnut honey and hazelnuts 30–1
herbs
    aubergine, black garlic, summer herbs 94
    spring garden salad 36
honey
    artichokes and honey 196
    pears, saffron, honey 172
    semolina, fennel and olive oil crackers, whipped ricotta,
        spicy honey, bee pollen 42–3
    Sicilian mango, lime, spicy honey and salt gelato 118
    smoked spring onions, chestnut honey and
        hazelnuts 30–1
    spicy honey 237
hummus, broad bean 233

I
infused vinegar 244
Italian sausages, pork *bombette*, radicchio,
    quince 168–9

J
Jerusalem artichoke chips 158–61
juniper berries: chicken liver pâté 136
jus, meat 235

K
kabocha squash soup, 'nduja red prawns 193
kimchi
    amberjack, citrus, kimchi 139
    kimchi butter 185
    kimchi tortellini, celeriac broth, kombu 146–9
kombu, kimchi tortellini, celeriac broth, 146–9
kumquats
    amberjack, citrus, kimchi 139
    citrus salad 204
kushiyaki, octopus, percoca, guanciale 108

L
lamb, mizuna and mustard seeds 60
lamb jus, red cabbage, orange, 162
lardo, sea bream, seared lettuce, 59
lavender: strawberry and lavender shrub 72
lemon curd, black olive and caramel tartlets with

liquorice 219–21

lemons

    candied citrus paste 234

    citronette 234

    citrus risotto 210

    lemon curd 219–21

    preserved lemons 240–1

    tomato risotto, garlic, lemon 106–7

lettuce: sea bream, seared lettuce, lardo 59

limes: Sicilian mango, lime, spicy honey and salt

    gelato 118

liquorice, lemon curd, black olive and caramel tartlets

    with 219–21

liver: chicken liver pâté 136

lunch 21

M

mackerel, raisin and caper sauce, bitter greens 215

mango: Sicilian mango, lime, spicy honey and salt gelato 118

Manu's tomato sauce 129

marmalade, grapefruit 227

mascarpone

    pea, wasabi, mascarpone tart 40

    whipped ricotta 42–3

mayonnaise, almond 232

meat jus 235

    pork *bombette*, radicchio, quince 168–9

melon, tomato and 92

milk

    crema gelato 216

    fig leaf gelato 120–1

    garlic emulsion 234–5

    Pecorino cheese fondu 236

    potato-skin gelato 170

mint: fava bean, sea urchin, mint risotto 54

miso: cuttlefish 'tagliatella', almond, miso, wild fennel 98–9

mizuna: lamb, mizuna and mustard seeds 60

monks beard, pickled garlic, candied citrus 38

Moroseta salad dressing 235–6

mozzarella, flat peach, cucumber, 82

mushrooms, pickled shiitake and cardoncelli 132–3

mustard seeds, lamb, mizuna and 60

N

nasturtiums, beef tartare, black garlic, daikon, 142

'nduja oil: kabocha squash soup, 'nduja red prawns 193

nectarines: white turnip, nectarine, green tomato aguachile 87

nutmeg, pumpkin and 156

nuts, asparagus and 34

O

octopus, percoca, guanciale kushiyaki 108

oils

    bay leaf oil 245

    garlic oil 245

    spicy oil 246

olive oil

    olive oil pan brioche 243

    semolina, fennel and olive oil crackers 42–3

olives: lemon curd, black olive and caramel tartlets with

    liquorice 219–21

onions

    chicken liver pâté 136

    croaker, onion, thyme 165

    meat jus 235

    pickled onions 240

    skirt steak, sour plum, pearl onions 111

    winter giardiniera 187

orange juice

    candied citrus paste 234

    red cabbage, orange, lamb jus 162

oranges

    citrus salad 204

    pickled fennel, rosemary, orange, and sun-dried tomatoes 225

oysters: barbecued oysters, spicy strawberry dressing 46

P

pan brioche

    fried eggs on toast with kimchi butter 185

    olive oil pan brioche 243

    pane e cioccolato 64

    tomato toast 88

pancetta, pumpkin and 156

pane e cioccolato 64

Parmesan cheese

    savoury crumble 242

    smoked potato plin, saffron beurre blanc 208–9

pasta

    braised rabbit tortellini, spring broth, wild garlic 50–3

    kimchi tortellini, celeriac broth, kombu 146–9

    pasta e ceci 206–7

    raviolo 'pane e pomodoro' in tomato broth 100–3

    smoked potato plin, saffron beurre blanc 208–9

pastry: pasta frolla 242–3

pâté, chicken liver 136

pea pods

    braised rabbit tortellini, spring broth, wild garlic 50–3

    gelato 118

peaches

    flat peach, cucumber, mozzarella 82

octopus, percoca, guanciale kushiyaki 108

peach galette 122–5

pears, saffron, honey 172

peas

braised rabbit tortellini, spring broth, wild garlic 50–3

pea, wasabi, mascarpone tart 40

Pecorino

Delica squash gnocchi, Pecorino, Jerusalem
artichoke 158–61

Pecorino cheese fondu 236

peppercorns, strawberry and 69

peppers: broad bean dumplings, pepper sauce 104

percoca: octopus, percoca, guanciale kushiyaki 108

pickles 240

pickled fennel, rosemary, orange, and sun-dried
tomatoes 225

pickled shiitake and cardoncelli mushrooms 132–3

winter giardiniera 187

plums: skirt steak, sour plum, pearl onions 111

polenta: *sbrisolona* with polenta, hazelnut, tangerine 177

pollen: fresh pollen gelato 118

pork

pork *bombette*, radicchio, quince 168–9

slow roasted pork shoulder, 5 spices, grape molasses 213

potatoes

Delica squash gnocchi, pecorino, Jerusalem
artichoke 158–61

potato-skin gelato 170

smoked potato plin, saffron beurre blanc 208–9

prawns, kabocha squash soup, 'nduja red 193

preserved lemons 240–1

pumpkin 155

flavour combinations 156

Q

quinces

pork *bombette*, radicchio, quince 168–9

smoked quince and five-spice shrub 180

R

rabbit

braised rabbit tortellini, spring broth, wild garlic 50–3

rabbit rillettes 190

radicchio: pork *bombette*, radicchio, quince 168–9

radishes: winter giardiniera 187

raisins: mackerel, raisin and caper sauce, bitter greens 215

raviolo 'pane e pomodoro' in tomato broth 100–3

red mullet in fig leaf 112

rice

brassica risotto 153

citrus risotto 210

fava bean, sea urchin, mint risotto 54

tomato risotto, garlic, lemon 106–7

ricotta

ricotta and bottarga gnocchi, anchovy brown butter
and bitter greens 56–7

whipped ricotta 42–3

rillettes, rabbit 190

risotto

brassica risotto 153

citrus risotto 210

fava bean, sea urchin, mint risotto 54

tomato risotto, garlic, lemon 106–7

rosemary: pickled fennel, rosemary, orange, and sun-dried
tomatoes 225

S

saffron

pears, saffron, honey 172

smoked potato plin, saffron beurre blanc 208–9

salads

citrus salad 204

flat peach, cucumber, mozzarella 82

spring garden salad 36

sauces & glazes 232–7

sausages: pork *bombette*, radicchio, quince 168–9

savoury crumble 242

sbrisolona with polenta, hazelnut, tangerine 177

sea bream, seared lettuce, lardo 59

sea urchins: fava bean, sea urchin, mint risotto 54

seafood, asparagus and 34

seaweed

asparagus and seaweed 34

kimchi tortellini, celeriac broth, kombu 146–9

semolina, fennel and olive oil crackers 42–3

sesame seeds: monks beard, pickled garlic, candied citrus 38

shiitake mushrooms: pickled shiitake and cardoncelli
mushrooms 132–3

shrubs

smoked quince and five-spice shrub 180

strawberry and lavender shrub 72

Sicilian mango, lime, spicy honey and salt gelato 118

skewers: octopus, percoca, guanciale kushiyaki 108

smoked potato plin, saffron beurre blanc 208–9

smoked quince and five-spice shrub 180

smoked spring onions, chestnut honey and hazelnuts 30–1

sorbet

apricot sorbet 120–1

cherry sorbet 118

strawberry, beetroot and chilli sorbet 71

cauliflower soup, egg yolk, buckwheat 203

celeriac and apple soup 144–5

kabocha squash soup, 'nduja red prawns 193

roasted vegetable gazpacho 80–1

sour plums: skirt steak, sour plum, pearl onions 111

soy sauce and wine glaze 236

spelt: apple, spelt and coriander cake 178

spice blends: warm spices 246

spicy honey 237

spicy oil 246

spicy strawberry dressing 46

spicy vinegar 245

spring 26–75

spring broth: braised rabbit tortellini, spring broth,
    wild garlic 50–3

spring garden salad 36

spring onions (scallions): smoked spring onions, chestnut
    honey and hazelnuts 30–1

squashes

    Delica squash gnocchi, pecorino, Jerusalem
        artichoke 158–61

    kabocha squash soup, 'nduja red prawns 193

squid tartare, wild sorrel sauce 49

strawberries 66

    flavour combinations 69

    spicy strawberry dressing 46

    spring garden salad 36

    strawberry and lavender shrub 72

    strawberry, beetroot and chilli sorbet 71

summer 76–129

T

'tagliatella': cuttlefish 'tagliatella', almond, miso,
    wild fennel 98–9

tahini

    grilled asparagus, gremolata and tahini sauce 28–9

    tahini sauce 237

tangerines: *sbrisolona* with polenta, hazelnut, tangerine 177

tartare

    beef tartare, black garlic, daikon, nasturtium 142

    squid tartare, wild sorrel sauce 49

tarts

    lemon curd, black olive and caramel tartlets with
        liquorice 219–21

    pea, wasabi, mascarpone tart 40

thyme, croaker, onion, 165

toast

    fried eggs on toast with kimchi butter 185

    tomato toast 88

tomatoes 91

flavour combinations 92

Manu's tomato sauce 129

pickled fennel, rosemary, orange, and sun-dried
    tomatoes 225

raviolo 'pane e pomodoro' in tomato broth 100–3

strawberries and tomatoes 69

tomato risotto, garlic, lemon 106–7

tomato toast 88

white turnip, nectarine, green tomato aguachile 87

tortellini

    braised rabbit tortellini, spring broth, wild garlic 50–3

    kimchi tortellini, celeriac broth, kombu 146–9

turnips: white turnip, nectarine, green tomato aguachile 87

V

vanilla, tomato and 92

vegetables

    pickled vegetables 240

    roasted vegetable gazpacho 80–1

    vegetable broth 241

    see also individual types of vegetable

vinaigrette 36, 112

    carpione vinaigrette 134

    toasted sesame vinaigrette 38

vinegar

    carpione vinegar 244

    elderflower vinegar 74

    infused vinegar 244

    spicy vinegar 245

W

wasabi: pea, wasabi, mascarpone tart 40

wild garlic, braised rabbit tortellini, spring broth, 50–3

wild sorrel: squid tartare, wild sorrel sauce 49

wine

    beurre blanc 232–3

    soy sauce and wine glaze 236

winter 182–229

winter giardiniera 187

Y

yoghurt

    pumpkin and yoghurt 156

    squid tartare, wild sorrel sauce 49

ACKNOWLEDGEMENTS

It feels unbelievable that I have really made it this far; the acknowledgement page is a bit like crossing the finish line after your first real marathon. If I have found the motivation, strength and persistence to make this possible, it is mainly thanks to the incredible support I received during this very difficult, exciting and unexpected process of writing my book.

Carlo: I can only start with you. It is incredible to think how it all started, a bit by chance, and where we got to. It has been a beautiful journey, always side by side. Thank you for always allowing me to be myself, for the constant support, for believing in my vision before I knew I had it. As we often repeat, we are only at the beginning.

Mum: You taught me all I know about the extraordinary ability to love through food. Thank you for everything, for your infinite patience, for the wonderful food you painted my childhood memory with, for comforting me when I was lost and pushing me when I needed it.

Chiara: I know it has not been easy to live with both me and this book for the last two years, putting up with my bad moods, uncertainties and constant second thoughts about basically everything. Thank you for your patience, for your true love, for willingly accepting that I am often lost in thoughts, for your comprehensive silences and for the life-saving midnight sandwiches.

My family: Dad, my brother Fabrizio, Aunt Rita, Aunt Irene and many others—thank you for always loving me, for accepting me with all my weirdness, for enthusiastically eating all my strange experiments and above all for the enormous trust and support I received so far.

Grandma Pina: You are my hero. I admire you when at 92 years old you continue to take care of your plants, take long walks in the park, cook polenta like there's no tomorrow, while videocalling your children with ease. You are my example of ultimate resilience and pure kindness.

Manu: This book is as much mine as it is yours. As I used to say, you are my right arm and my left one, too. In five years of working together we have been through a lot, always trying to improve ourselves, delving into the heart of cooking. Thank you for trusting me, for the hard work, for accepting the toughest challenges and for the pure dedication. And now, let's have a negroni.

Giulia: Thank you for supporting me on this long journey. For analysing every detail, every word and every image, for responding to all my texts with intelligent and honest comments. I am so lucky to have you as my best friend, or as we always say, sister.

Andrew: Thank you for creating such a wonderful place that I have the great fortune to call home. Your clean and simple vision inspires me every day.

My friends: Beatrice, Matteo, Alessio, Antony, Chiara, Martina, Marcelo, Marco, Stefano, Riccardo, Luca, Eva and all of you. Thank you for being there, you are that magic combination of fuel, lifeline, fun, laughter and roots.

My Moroseta family: Alessio, Anete, Valeria, Nicola, Marcella, Piera, Matteo and many more. I am so lucky to share my day-to-day with you, to be able to call you family. Thank you for the understanding, the trust, the laughter, the coffee breaks and the heartfelt chats at the end of the day.

Moroseta kitchen: Laura, Imma, Riccardo, Maria, Danilo, Joaquim, Daniel, Benedetta and all of you who have crossed the threshold of that kitchen over the last eight years, sharing a little of this extraordinary journey. Thank you for everything, simply without your hard work and fundamental contribution, I would not be where I am and I would not be the person I am now. Thank you for believing in my vision, for giving something of your own, for creating a kitchen environment where we can feel free and safe.

Alice: You were the first person to give me a chance to express myself in a professional kitchen, making me realise that there was a place for someone like me, despite my very basic skills and technical gaps. Thank you for your trust, encouragement, long walks in nature, sincere advice and genuine laughter.

Beloved suppliers: Luca and Mate, Antonio, Francesco, Vito, Giuseppe, Michele and all of you. My job would be boring and quite meaningless without you, cooking with your products makes me fall in love with this profession every day, thank you for the incredible work you do.

Eve: Amazing editor of this book. Thank you for guiding me, for understanding, for listening to all my anxieties, for being incredibly patient and truly understanding. Thank you for being always there, for reassuring me and for making all this possible.

Stephen: You visualised this book before it existed. Thank you for giving me the time to understand it and accept it, for your gentle guidance and invaluable trust.

Maureen: It is an honour to have your photos in this book, you managed to enter our world with delicacy, sensitivity and enthusiasm. I felt truly understood and represented by your images. Thank you for your sincere care, for your unique and intimate vision, for immediately becoming family, for being involved from day one.

Letizia: I asked you to jump on this project a bit last minute, in a moment of difficulty when I did not know how to get out of it. With your delicacy, comprehension and tenacity, we solved everything, producing an incredible number of images in just a few days in the scorching heat of the Apulian summer. Thank you for always understanding me, for listening to my tangled thoughts and for following me in the most absurd situations.

Tegan: You have interpreted my world into the graphic design I have always dreamed of, achieving that perfect combination of simple, elegant, unfussy, distinctive and clear. Thank you for your hard work, patience and for doing a million cover tests.

Linda: I am honoured to have your wonderful ceramics in this book. You immediately understood what I was looking for, there was no need for briefings or reference images, blindly trusting your vision was the right choice I could have made. Thank you for all your art, for bringing it to me personally travelling through Italy, for all the brutal beauty you have concentrated in this project.

Antonella: I have always dreamt of a large marble surface to cook on, thank you for making it possible for this project.

Romano: The simplicity of your linen was the only props I needed. Thank you for your flamboyant personality, for being dedicated to the project and for the miles of beautiful fabric.

Editorial team: A heartfelt thank you to all the Hardie Grant team who made all this possible.

ABOUT THE AUTHOR

Born in Milan in 1989, Giorgia Eugenia Goggi has always had a huge curiosity for all things food. After graduating from a fashion degree, Giorgia worked in the industry before turning her attention to the professional kitchen. She won her first internship at a Japanese restaurant in Milan, and then worked at many highly regarded restaurants in London and Copenhagen before arriving at Moroseta in June 2017. What started as a short summer residency in the kitchen and becoming caretaker of a little vegetable garden has become an eight-year journey to the making of a much-lauded destination restaurant. She lives in the Puglian countryside with her partner and two cats, Lucio and Atena, pursuing the dream of a laid-back life among citrus trees, lots of books, wine and dinners with friends.

Published in 2024 by Hardie Grant Books (London)

Hardie Grant Books (London)
5th & 6th Floors
52–54 Southwark Street
London SE1 1UN

hardiegrantbooks.com

Publishing Director: Kajal Mistry
Commissioning Editor: Eve Marleau
Design: Tegan Ella Hendel
Recipe Development: Giorgia Eugenia Goggi and Emmanuel Gavezzoli
Copy Editor: Tara O'Sullivan
Proofreader: Kate Wanwimolruk
Indexer: Vanessa Bird
Photography: Maureen Evans and Letizia Cigliutti
Production Controller: Martina Georgieva

Ceramics: Amoraw Studio, Martina Geroni (pages 179 and 198), and KANA (pages 202 and 47).
Textiles: Arno Studio
Marble Surfaces: Marmi Azzolini
Additional Locations: Casa Maiora, Solequp Organic Gardens

British Library Cataloguing-in-Publication Data.
A catalogue record for this book is available from the British Library.

Moroseta Kitchen
ISBN: 978-1-78488-537-3

10 9 8 7 6 5 4 3 2 1

Colour reproduction by p2d
Printed and bound in China by Leo Paper Products Ltd.